A man comes across an ancient enemy, beaten and left for dead. He lifts the wounded man onto the back of a donkey and takes him to an inn to tend to the man's recovery. Jesus tells this story and instructs those who are listening to "go and do likewise."

Likewise books explore a compassionate, active faith lived out in real time. When we're skeptical about the status quo, Likewise books challenge us to create culture responsibly. When we're confused about who we are and what we're supposed to be doing, Likewise books help us listen for God's voice. When we're discouraged by the troubled world we've inherited, Likewise books encourage us to hold onto hope.

In this life we will face challenges that demand our response. Likewise books face those challenges with us so we can act on faith.

LIKEWISE.　　*Go and do.*

THE NEW FRIARS

The Emerging Movement Serving the World's Poor

Scott A. Bessenecker

IVP Books

An imprint of InterVarsity Press
Downers Grove, Illinois

InterVarsity Press
P.O. Box 1400, Downers Grove, IL 60515-1426
World Wide Web: www.ivpress.com
E-mail: mail@ivpress.com

InterVarsity Press® is the book-publishing division of InterVarsity Christian Fellowship/USA®, a student movement active on campus at hundreds of universities, colleges and schools of nursing in the United States of America, and a member movement of the International Fellowship of Evangelical Students. For information about local and regional activities, write Public Relations Dept., InterVarsity Christian Fellowship/USA, 6400 Schroeder Rd., P.O. Box 7895, Madison, WI 53707-7895, or visit the IVCF website at <www.intervarsity.org>.

Scripture quotations, unless otherwise noted, are from the New Revised Standard Version of the Bible, copyright 1989 by the Division of Christian Education of the National Council of the Churches of Christ in the USA. Used by permission. All rights reserved.

Design: Cindy Kiple

Images: open hands: Peter Holst/Getty Images
      old shoes: Karen Beard/Getty Images
      holding hands: Richard Beebe/istockphoto.com
      Sharmila Blair and Riny: Sharmona Owen
      little boy: Ash Barker

All other photographs, unless otherwise indicated, are from the author.
Interior artwork is used by permission of the artists.

ISBN-10: 0-8308-3601-2
ISBN-13: 978-0-8308-3601-7

Printed in the United States of America ∞

Library of Congress Cataloging-in-Publication Data

Bessenecker, Scott.
  The new friars: the emerging movement serving the world's poor
/ by Scott Bessenecker.
    p. cm.
  Includes bibliographical references.
  ISBN-13: 978-0-8308-3601-7 (pbk.: alk. paper)
  ISBN-10: 0-8308-3601-2 (pbk.: alk. paper)
  1. Church work with the poor. 2. Poverty—Religious aspects
—Christianity. 3. Commitment (Psychology)—Religious aspects
—Christianity. 4. Missions—Theory. 5. Monastic and religious
life. 6. Vows. I. Title. BV639.P6B47 2006 261.8'325—dc22

                                                  2006020897

| P | 18 | 17 | 16 | 15 | 14 | 13 | 12 | 11 | 10 | 9 | 8 | 7 | 6 | 5 | 4 | 3 |
| Y | 21 | 20 | 19 | 18 | 17 | 16 | 15 | 14 | 13 | 12 | 11 | 10 | 09 | 08 |

For Janine

CONTENTS

ACKNOWLEDGMENTS

I have wanted to write this book for a long time now. In fact, more than three years ago I wrote several chapters and an outline. A publisher took my book proposal pretty seriously, but after an initial face-to-face meeting they turned it down, feeling like it appealed to too narrow a market niche. Nobody would buy it, so the reasoning went. That meeting knocked the wind out of me, and it took a couple years before I had the energy to pick up my pen again.

That original assessment—that this material will have a limited appeal—may well prove to be right. Indeed, I have no idea, standing here at the front end of publication, whether very many people will be interested in what I believe is an extremely potent but admittedly small phenomenon.

Doubts have been my constant companion in this journey. Is God really stirring up another movement of preaching orders to serve the world's most destitute residents? Is it really fair to call these slum-dwelling missionaries "friars"? They do not come under any one denomination or church structure, and seem to be creating a variety of mission agencies and organizations. Do they truly compare favorably with the likes of Franciscan, Jesuit and Celtic orders?

More troubling still is the question of whether I am qualified to write such a book. That familiar voice always seems to be so close at hand. "Who do you think you are? You've not lived long-term in a slum community like those of whom you write. What are your credentials? You are only a poser, and have no right to tell the stories of those who live more radically."

But at a certain point it took more energy not to write this book than to simply let it all spill out onto paper. Jim, my boss and the director of the Urbana Student Mission Convention, gave my muddled first chapters to his wife, Beth, who saw promise in them. I am grateful for the risk Jim took in promoting this book for Urbana 2006. It is largely due to Jim and Beth's support for this manuscript that it now rests in your hands.

Many others along the way have helped to buoy my flagging spirits. Thanks, Randy, for urging me to pick up my pen again when I was discouraged, and then sojourning with me in this process from start to finish. Jill and Heidi, we have been yoked together in this ministry in such a way that this is as much your book as it is mine. Roy and Becky, you two have consistently been there to fan my flickering flame. Thanks, Dad, for letting me tell a hard part of your story and for the ways you and Margaret spurred me on with your words of encouragement after reading my first draft. Mom, my brothers and sisters and the entire Hillsman clan—what a privilege to be surrounded by people who think more highly of me than I deserve. My editor at InterVarsity Press, Dave, and the four mystery readers who provided page-by-page feedback, along with Tom, Bill, Carrie, Mike and some of those aforementioned—your constructive critique was so instrumental in helping to shape this material that I am almost embarrassed by my first draft. Janine, Gary and Grete, your artwork on the "old friars" is beautiful. Thanks for pouring your hearts into those pieces. I'm also impossibly indebted to my church family at Faith Community Bible Church; your compassionate love for the broken things of this world, your zeal for true intimacy with Jesus and your discontent with the status quo is helping to shape who I am becoming.

To those of you who, for love of Jesus and the poor have taken up residence in places of unbelievable poverty, crime and despair: you are my heroes. Thanks particularly to those of you who let me tell a piece of your story in *The New Friars*. The little recognition you may receive as a result of this book is nothing in comparison to how the Savior will boast, dance and shout over you when this life is over.

Hannah, Philip and Laura, you three give me such hope for the future. If you are any indication of the generation to come, then this world has something to look forward to. And, of course, there is you, Janine, to whom this book is dedicated. We've been together since we were teenagers; so long I've nearly forgotten what life is like without you. You have seen me at my obsessive-compulsive, passive-aggressive, self-absorbed worst, and yet have never stopped supporting me, challenging me and cheering me on. Thank you.

1   GOD'S RECURRING DREAM

When I was in high school my younger brother, Chris, and I decided to visit a Franciscan monastery in Davenport, Iowa. We were young and idealistic; both of us took pretty seriously our Catholic heritage, and we were curious about this gathering of men who would pledge themselves to poverty in order to stand alongside the poor—helping not so much by lifting up the poor from above but by placing themselves underneath the poor, so as to push them up from below.

The idea of living in a vow-driven community seemed enormous and maybe a bit exciting. This was different from being a priest; the Franciscan vows wed you to poverty and to Christ in a missional way. Was this a calling we could endure: to be single all our lives, poor and devoted to the authority of the church?

At the time I was not really aware of the beginnings of the order—of St. Francis of Assisi camping out in San Damiano, a dilapidated chapel in the advanced stages of disintegration; of his association with lepers; of the punishment his body endured through his extreme denial of most any comfort. The vows of celibacy and submission to the authority of the church were not the thing that drew Chris and me to the monastery. It was the Franciscan ideal of rejecting the materialistic life and serving the poor: turning one's back on the "American Dream" and a life of conspicuous consumption, and turning toward God's dream of a life of simplicity and compassion toward society's rejects. With a healthy dose of respect we entered the sacred grounds.

I'm not exactly sure what Chris and I expected, but it certainly wasn't the college fraternity environment we encountered. As we met some of the brothers who had gathered in a well-groomed dining room for a meal and a smoke, we sensed that this group of men lived differently than the homeless men who first gathered around Francis in the early part of the thirteenth century. The brothers swore like sailors, smoked like chimneys and lived like kings, so far as Chris and I could observe.

The swearing and smoking, which so offended my religious sensibilities at the time, I have since come to peace with. But what troubles me to this day was the relative wealth of this order of brothers in comparison to my middle-class family. We asked the brother leading us on this tour of the monastery about the cable TV in every room. This was 1979 when cable was a relatively new luxury—one that our middle-class family did not enjoy. "The brothers take a vow of *personal* poverty," our guide emphasized. "These things are actually owned by the monastery, not the brothers." Apparently, as long as it was communal wealth, at this monastery a Franciscan could live in luxury.

I suppose the thing that really jarred me and Chris was the baby baptismal in the backyard, which had been turned into a barbecue pit for pleasant summer evenings when these "friends of the poor" would enjoy a grilled steak with their beer and cigarettes as they rehashed the games they had watched on ESPN earlier that day.

Maybe I had overly romanticized the Franciscans, but the things I thought were noble and righteous about the church seemed like a façade. Underneath the austere Franciscan robe, tied with the simplicity of a rope belt, was a rich kid who simply got around the vow of poverty by enjoying someone else's wealth.

THE FRANCISCAN SPIRIT

The Davenport monastery has since closed down. Certainly the Franciscan spirit is alive and well within the Catholic church; there are truly self-sacrificing Franciscan orders, along with its sister movement the Poor Clare orders, all over the world. One Franciscan priest I met in San Francisco has opened his church to the homeless and lives as close to the Franciscan ideal as anyone I know. So the Davenport monastery may not have been representative of the Franciscan order. But that visit during my high-school years was profoundly disenfranchising for me.

Twenty-five years later I found myself visiting a twenty-four-year-old evangelical who had recently graduated from MIT. With a world of wealth open to him, David Von Stroh instead chose to move to a Bangkok slum community. He lived in a scrap-wood structure in an upper room over a space where the church in that community gathered. His dwelling, like the others in his community, was built on stilts over the raw sewage that ran below the neighborhood of corrugated-tin lean-tos. David was working with this community as an insider trying to identify the key felt needs of their slum neighborhood. Addressing the problems of drug use is at the top of their list. The woman in the structure next to David runs methamphetamines out of her home to addicts and dealers in the area.

David Von Stroh, holding a child in Bangkok

David was struggling with the loneliness that comes with the kind of life he had chosen—to live among the poor as one of them, in a foreign country where he was struggling to learn the language and build friendships. He does not have the same sort of prestige that often accompanies the outward appearance of pious poverty, but David is living closer to the spirit of St. Francis than the brothers Chris and I visited in Davenport, Iowa.

It is one of God's recurring dreams to raise up servants intent upon reaching those who have been impoverished materially, spiritually and emotionally—those people who have been forgotten, abused and rejected. There are many churches and missional movements that began with fiery passion, founded by wild-eyed youth to minister to such neglected communities as coal miners or street kids. But visionary Christian movements to the world's margins have been born and subsequently died dozens of times through the ages. Some of the idealistic fervor of such revolutionary movements has been lost in many quarters of the church today, overshadowed by an obsession with self-improvement and accumulation, and an acquiescence to the shopping mall mentality.

I believe we are at the front edge of another missional, monastic-like order made up of men and women, many of whom are in their twenties and thirties, burning with a passion to serve the destitute in slum communities of the developing world—not from a position of power but from alongside them, living in the same makeshift housing, breathing the same sewage-tainted air, subject to the same government bulldozers that threaten to raze their communities. They are new friars, flying just below our radar because they have not come under any single denominational or suprachurch banner.

These communities are carried forward in their mission through the agency of solemn vows or commitments made to God, just as the missionary monastic orders of old. These vows rule their conduct, their community and their ministry.

THE NAZIRITE VOW

Vows are practically unheard of in twenty-first-century Western society. Marriage vows are about all we have left, and they're not holding up too well. Many people are begging someone to set the bar higher, to call them to uncommon levels of commitment and devotion.

In God's economy, vows have always been critical. As far back as ancient Israel, God used vow-driven individuals and communities to accomplish his purposes. When women or men wanted to make vows to him, he seemed delighted to oblige them. God consistently culled out from the ranks of his people a few who would stick out, act out and speak out. God gave opportunity for those outside of the priesthood to set themselves apart for acts of devotion and service to him—a kind of voluntarily ostracism. The prophets were of this ilk, as were certain leaders like Moses the deliverer, Deborah the judge or David the king. Each was upholding as much a religious calling as a political one.

In God's economy, vows have always been critical.

The Old Testament law specified a way by which anybody could set himself or herself apart: the Nazirite vow. If you look beyond the cloistered, celibate image of monasticism and instead see a group of individuals who have voluntarily set themselves apart for uncommon lives of service and devotion to God, you might say that Nazirites were a kind of ancient Jewish monk or nun.

In Numbers 6 God prescribes some ways that these men and women might be distinguished not only from the common residents of Israel but from the priestly class. Nazirites were not to touch or be touched by three things.

- They could not come near or touch a dead body.
- No product of the grapevine or any fermented drink was to touch their lips.
- No razor was to touch their head.

So the Nazirites were teetotalers with dreadlocks who stayed away from funerals. They were to shave their head at the beginning and the end of their vow, but in between they were to keep away from scissors.

In the little agrarian communities that typified the ancient world, these characteristics were just the sort of things that would make a person stick out. It would be hard to imagine a month without some kind of celebration that included wine or grapes. And in an extended community without mortuaries and funeral homes, touching a dead body would be far more commonplace than it is today. But God wanted to allow a handful of people to ostracize themselves from the wider community of Israel for the sake of making a solemn commitment to him. He wanted them to be recognized as men and women who had made a vow.

What is interesting to note is the gender-inclusiveness of the Nazirite vow. The priesthood was exclusively a male office; women, however, could be Nazirites (Numbers 6:2). What's more, the nature of the vow and period of the vow seem to be up to the vow-maker. The apostle Paul appears to have made a Nazirite vow at two points in his ministry (Acts 18:18; 21:23-26). One of those periods, Acts 21, was done in concert with four others, so apparently there could be Nazirite communities.

Several biblical Nazirites had a lifelong calling. Samson and Samuel were pledged as Nazirites by their mothers, and John the Baptizer was made a Nazirite by order of an angelic visitation to his father. Each of them fulfilled their vows their whole lives. Samson was set apart to be a deliverer, Samuel as a judge and John as one who would prepare the way for Jesus. These were not just "New Year's resolution" sort of commitments, they were people set apart for a mission that would require intense levels of devotion—a dedicated separation.

When Martin Luther left the Augustinian order of monks and eventually condemned the making of vows, he may have left the Protestant movement bereft of a God-ordained function to set oneself apart not for the ministry of raising up and caring for a local church (though that is an important calling) but for focused communities of men and women with defined, disciplined devotion and a particular mission. I believe there have been in each generation those who long to gather with like-minded individuals to be set apart in service guided by a rule, order or set of disciplines. In fact, I would go so far as to say that there are places on earth that cannot be truly changed by the kingdom of God without people willing to make Nazirite-like commitments. Call them new friars, twenty-first-century monks and nuns, modern Nazirites or radically charged missionaries, but there is something happening today that follows a long established pattern of movements of vow-driven Christians directed to the social and geographic fringe.

A HISTORIC PATTERN

Missionary statesman Ralph Winter breaks nearly all of human history into "supercenturies," suggesting that the church experiences unprecedented growth about every four hundred years. Gaining his inspiration from Kenneth Scott Latourette's *A History of Christianity*, Winter sees five critical renaissances in the two thousand years since Jesus lived, died and rose again:

- the Classical Renaissance (A.D. 400)
- the Carolingian Renaissance (A.D. 800)
- the Medieval Renaissance (A.D. 1200)
- the Reformation and Counter-Reformation (A.D. 1600)
- the Evangelical Renaissance, which Winter believes is beginning in our time

This two-thousand-year-old pattern has been powered mainly by youth. In each period, radically motivated men and women moved to the fringe and pressed the church into the social and geographic edges. In the first renaissance it was the Celtic and Augustinian monks, in the second it was the Benedictine and Nestorian monks, in the third the Franciscans and Dominicans, and in the fourth the Jesuits, Moravians and Anabaptists. What we are seeing today, with the emergence of the new friars, is a continuation of this pattern of mission orders—devotional communities that are high on ministry to the outcasts.

The historic orders share a number of things in common. To make a fair comparison of those movements to the emerging movement, we must look beyond practices I consider ascetic extremes—things like submerging oneself in an icy stream upon encountering a lustful thought or self-flagellation (though I have no doubt the new friars might practice those things if they proved helpful in growing more intimate with Christ or successful in their mission). Instead we must ask ourselves, what are the essential ingredients that make these orders unique and set them apart from the ordinary practices of the faith?

Incarnational. First and foremost, these orders were *incarnational.* They sought not simply to *bring* the gospel to the lost or oppressed from the outside, as if by remote control, but to *be* the gospel by becoming part of the communities of dispossessed they sought to serve. They took their cues from God, who, rather than saving humanity by asking us to become like him, chose instead to become like us. The incarnation of God in the man Jesus Christ served as the foundational missiology and modus operandi of the old orders. When the Jesuits donned the garb of Confucius scholars or the Moravians considered the possibility of selling themselves into slavery in Jamaica, they were only following in the footsteps of their Master.

> **They sought not simply to *bring* the gospel to the lost or oppressed but to *be* the gospel.**

Devotional. Second, these orders were radically *devotional.* In the Augustinian order, correcting a brother who was sinning and in denial was an act of compassion:

> If your brother, for example, were suffering a bodily wound that he wanted to hide for fear of undergoing treatment, would it not be cruel of you to remain silent and a mercy on your part to make this known? How much greater then is your obligation to make his condition known lest he continue to suffer a more deadly wound of the soul.

Each order was organized around a set of spiritual commitments, or a "rule," to govern their walk with Jesus, with one another and with the community of lost, poor or broken souls into which they had grafted themselves. They vowed themselves to principles of holiness and purity that went beyond the common practices of the faith, then held each other to these ideals quite rigidly.

Communal. Third, these orders were *communal,* living together and sharing many of those things that they held privately before joining the order.

I'm not speaking of personal luxury items simply renamed *communal* luxury items. Given their commitment to incarnation, most of these communities were quite austere. I'm talking instead about living in a way that goes beyond the principle of the single-family dwelling, where traditional Western society begins and ends its understanding of a shared property.

These men and women moved into a community of mostly strangers and lived as a family. They committed themselves to one another out of love. The Rule of St. Clare, for the female Franciscans, speaks of the communal commitment in this way: "If a mother loves and cherishes her child according to the flesh, how much more diligently should a sister love and cherish her sister according to the Spirit." The abbess of the convent was to be

> attentive to her sisters as a good mother is to her daughters, and let her take care especially to provide for them according to the needs of each one out of the alms that the Lord shall give. Let her also be so kind and available that they may safely reveal their needs and confidently have recourse to her at any hour, as they see fit both for themselves and their sisters.

Missional. Fourth, the historic orders were *missional*—at least the ones that went to communities on the *geographic* fringe. These were communities on the move, responsible for stretching the borders of the church into the dark corners of Europe. Celtic monks, for instance, were known to board a small boat, raise the sail and pray that God would direct their vessel to some barbarian tribe where the gospel had not been heard.

The cloistered (or inward) and the missional (or outward) forces in these various monastic communities were often held in tension, some emphasizing one over the other. Likewise today we find both cloistered and missional communities cropping up. The New Monasticism, as it is being called, often consists of households of Christian men and women planted in dying inner-city communities within their home country, attempting to live the Christian ideal among their neighbors, drawing the lost, poor and broken to themselves. They resemble more the cloistered order. The new friars, on the other hand, have something of the spirit of mission-driven monks and nuns in them, leaving their mother country and moving to those parts of the world where little is known about Jesus.

Marginal. Finally, these movements were *marginal.* This is true in two respects: they were on the fringe of the mainstream church; and they sought to plant themselves among people who existed on the edges of society.

Almost all of the movements discussed in *The New Friars* have been born out of a reaction to spiritual flabbiness in the broader church and a tendency to assimilate into a corrupt, power-hungry world. The movements were started by people possessed of a holy discontent—discontent with a church who had succumbed to the very self-absorption it was commissioned to combat. These men and women found it necessary to hold themselves to a higher standard from what had become traditional church life in order to pursue something more idyllic. The *vita apostolica* it was sometimes called—the apostolic life.

In the process of pursuing a different kind of spiritual life, they often found company with those who were trapped outside the systems that kept the powerful powerful and the rich rich. They positioned themselves alongside social lepers, economic slaves and political malcontents on the world's margins, and often found themselves on the margins of the church as a result. Nestorians, for example, were considered heretics by what was at the time mainstream Christianity for emphasizing the human attributes of Christ as distinct from his divine attributes. They were pushed out of the Western stream of the church and established friendships with the enemies of the Roman Empire. They served among the Persian shahs and Mongol khans and were often on the other side of political conflicts in which the church of the West was caught up. To this day the Nestorian movement is mostly unknown to the mainstream church.

Martin Luther is credited with saying, "The church may be a whore, but she's my mother." Despite the fact that these movements were set apart from the local expressions of church, and even sometimes at odds with it, they loved and served the majority church community. Church historian Adolf Harnack says,

It was always the monks who saved the Church when sinking, emancipated her when becoming enslaved to the world, defended her when assailed. These it was that kindled hearts that were growing cold, bridled refractory spirits, recovered for the church alienated nations.

I predict that the emerging movement to the world's poor, powered by new friars, will also bring renewal to the global church of the twenty-first century.

NEW FRIAR COMMUNITIES

Viv Grigg, a young man from New Zealand, moved into a squatter settlement in Manila, Philippines, in the 1970s, living out a radical form of incarnational mission. In the 1980s and 1990s he churned out a string of books and articles calling the church to make room for Protestant missionary orders among the urban poor. Vows would play a key role, he explained, if these servant movements were to be effective: "Workers with [these movements] make covenants to live lifestyles of non-destitute poverty and simplicity for the sake of identification with the poor." Grigg went so far as to call young people to vows of singleness, at least for a season:

> The Protestant ethic, in its reaction to an errant Catholicism, coupled with the breakdown of American family structures, has moved to an extreme worship of comfortable marriage that ignores the pressing urgency of the times and sacrifices needed to redeem the poor of the earth.

Grigg was calling the church to grant people the option to devote themselves to a kind of missionizing monastic order. Since the 1980s, a few idealistic Western youth, some of them inspired by Grigg, have begun forming organizations committed to living lives of holiness in the world's slum communities. Most of these organizations have struggled with the word *order,* wondering if it appropriately defines who they are. It smells musty and old, yet describes better than most words the unique combination of communal orientation, quest for holiness and incarnational engagement in mission at the margins. Not all of these groups have chosen to register their works as

religious orders, nor have they placed themselves under the authority of the
Catholic Church (though all of them have in their ranks, or at least are open
to receiving, practicing Catholics as part of their communities). But each of
them possesses the five qualities that put them squarely in the tradition of
historic, mission-driven monks and nuns: they are each incarnational, communal, devotional, missional and marginal.

- **InnerCHANGE** identifies itself as a Christian order and is composed of
  communities of missionaries living and ministering incarnationally
  among the poor. They wed the contemplative, prophetic and missionary
  traditions of the church.

- **Servant Partners** is another organization of missionaries living and
  working among the poor. Missionaries with Servant Partners must be
  prepared "to die to ourselves in all areas of life: finances, possessions,
  housing, decision-making, and ministry opportunities. . . . Instead of
  seeking status and honor among our peers, we must look to be servants."

- **Servants to Asia's Urban Poor (Servants)** live in the slum communities
  of Asian megacities, working with the poor to bring renewal, hope and
  justice to their cities. Rather than beginning their own churches, Servants
  prefers to work under the authority of existing churches in the slums.
  They seek to learn from and contribute to national Christian pastors and
  leaders in the cities where their communities are planted.

- **Urban Neighbours of Hope (UNOH)** defines itself as a mission order
  among the poor. Reflecting on the historic orders of the church, UNOH's
  leaders state, "We believe God is again responding to a reshaped reality
  with a new breed of gospel orders."

- **Word Made Flesh (WMF),** according to executive director Chris
  Heuertz, is simply a collection of broken people. They are also young: the
  "grandfather" of WMF's work in Romania, David Chronic, is thirty-two.
  He founded the work in Galati, Romania, when he was twenty-three.
  This is the norm for a mission whose members range in age from twenty-
  two to thirty-six.

Chris Heuertz, center, executive director of Word Made Flesh

There are, of course, followers of Jesus who were born in the harsh realities of urban poverty and who seek to follow him there. One organization working with the urban poor, Kairos, for instance, was born out of the barrios of Brazil. The church is, after all, predominantly a church of the southern hemisphere and located squarely in the developing world. Those who grew up in the developing world and are now serving the urban poor in other parts of the world deserve a book all their own. The interesting thing about these five organizations based in the West, however, is that many of their missionaries have sought a path of downward mobility—moving from places of power and influence to places of poverty and desperation, renouncing privilege and opportunity in the West in order to find "true religion," as James puts it, among the orphans and widows in slum communities: "Religion that is pure and undefiled before God, the Father, is this: to care for orphans and widows in their distress, and to keep oneself unstained by the world" (James 1:27).

As for me, I want to draw near to these twenty-first-century monks and nuns because the Spirit of God is moving through them as they impact the lowest strata of human life. Celibacy and asceticism are not necessarily part of the new friar movement, nor is unquestioned devotion to a hierarchical church structure. But these men and women do embrace sacrifice and suffering, and they are committed to Christ and his church in radically humble ways. It is imperative that the broader community of believers release and support this movement of saints intent on pouring out their lives for people on the fringe. That is the focus of *The New Friars*, and that is why I have written this book.

To begin, however, we must go to the world's fringe, where the modern lepers, slaves and outcasts are attracting these new friars just as they did the historic mission-driven nuns and monks. From these dark and seemingly Godforsaken corners of our world, the church's renaissance has almost always sprouted, as if God was hiding there, waiting for a few of his people to join him in the unveiling of a fresh renaissance. So it is in the slum communities of our megacities that we will start, asking ourselves how in the world so many people have gotten trapped into such desperate circumstances, and how God might be calling his people to respond.

PUSHED INTO POVERTY

Sleepless

Thoughts wash ashore
Lapping up to the toes of my memory
Half a world and a week away
    I walk the streets of Saigon.

Next to me
my son
Retrieved at midnight for reasons
    my foggy brain can't quite recall
    foot in my ribs, reminding me he's there

I see a boy his age in Saigon
Naked, except for a dirty shirt
    lying before the iron bars of a storefront.

Awake
No hope of sleep
Two boys prod me
One foot in my ribs
    and one in my conscience.

"Look at me," they say.
"I am someone."
"I am here."

My first encounter with a slum community was in 1995. I was in Ho Chi Minh City (formerly Saigon), Vietnam. It wasn't really much of an encounter. I simply looked across a canal at a row of corrugated-tin and scrap-wood single-story structures. They were a dense jumble of discarded materials that formed a kind of neighborhood. But this neighborhood was unlike any I'd seen up to that point. Naked kids played in dirty water, and the trash that surrounded them seemed to melt into the backdrop of this community.

Ho Chi Minh City

The slum got in the way of my viewing experience. It got in the way of some of the more externally pleasing aspects of Saigon. More upsetting still, it got in the way of my conscience.

TRACTABLE AND INTRACTABLE POVERTY

The Permsup slum community in Bangkok, Thailand, where Dave Von Stroh lives is in the way too. The government wants to build a highway, but the four hundred families of Permsup have their homes, such as they are, planted right along the path where the transportation authorities are determined to construct their road.

This kind of thing happens all the time. Governments and developers find slum communities a bother, an eyesore, an urban deformity. But they are neighborhoods. They are fellowships of men, women and children, just like the neighborhoods where the nonpoor live. At least the Thai government is giving the Permsup community some warning. They have two years to find another place. Other slum communities aren't so lucky. Damayan Lagi is a slum community in Manila, Philippines. In the 1980s New Zealander Michael Duncan, along with his family, moved into Damayan Lagi as an act of worship and mission, working with Servants to Asia's Urban Poor. Their slum was burned to the ground (allegedly by a rich developer who wanted to build townhouses for the wealthy) with the same sort of attitude one might have when exterminating a pest.

Most of the time when a squatter community is set ablaze or is razed by bulldozers, or when a government shuts down a garbage dump that has become the home of hundreds of scavenger families, the people who are displaced simply find another site on which to resurrect their neighborhood. There they remain until they're in the way of another force whose engines drown out their voices while flattening their community.

The slum-dwelling new friars are developing a rudimentary knowledge of what it is that makes the poor poor, especially since they have bound themselves to the desperately poor and face the same stark realities of life that they do. The Duncan family helped organize their community to act, breaking out of the cycles of victimization under which they suffered. At this writing David Von Stroh is helping the Permsup community save money communally in order to buy property together and not be at the mercy of developers and transportation authorities.

There are tractable and intractable forms of poverty—poverty you can break out of and poverty you can't. The communities to which the Duncan family and David Von Stroh have attached themselves suffer an intractable form of poverty. A poverty so entrenched that, generations later, the grandchildren of the impoverished are impoverished themselves with no sign of breaking free. However, most middle-class and rich folk, like those of us who can afford to spend fifteen dollars on a book, can find tractable poverty in our past without looking too hard. It's the kind of poverty where systems are in place that allow determined, poor families to climb out, even if it takes a generation.

THE POOR IN MY PAST

My dad grew up poor. Small-town Iowa poor. His father worked for the railroad but somehow just could not make ends meet. While many suburban Americans in the 1950s were experiencing a prosperity boom, the Besseneckers didn't have flush toilets. By the time child number eight was on the way, Grandpa Bessenecker was an alcoholic and had emotionally checked out. He divorced Grandma, moved across the Mississippi River to Rock Island, Illinois, and got a job driving a cab. My dad didn't see his father again until Grandpa was on his deathbed twenty-five years later, suffering from cancer of the larynx.

As the oldest kid, Dad became the de facto father figure. He helped raise his seven brothers and sisters while trying to keep up with school. His mom worked hard to earn next to nothing and managed to hold the family together. Dad speaks of his father's abandonment with a lot of pain. He has since learned to forgive him, even to fix his memories onto sweeter times when his dad was just poor, not poor and captive to alcohol. He understands something of the hardships that drove his father to drink—the loss of dignity that not being able to provide for your family produces in a person. Despair finds temporary rest in alcohol only to wake more despairing than before. The codependence of despair and alcohol is what stole the life from my grandfather.

It's harder for my dad's brothers and sisters to make peace with their father. Only the oldest kids have much of a memory of their dad at all. They grew up in a single-parent home under fairly bleak circumstances with their dad living nearby but choosing not to have a relationship with them. But despite being born into scarcity, most of the Iowa Besseneckers have managed to pull themselves into the middle class—or close enough to it. The marks of poverty have not completely disappeared, but only one of the kids seemed to get caught in the poverty undertow. Nearly all of that generation of Besseneckers have obtained an education, held decent jobs and raised relatively functional families who have avoided the serious level of economic deprivation into which they were born. Looking back on their harsh circumstances now, it is quite a testimony to my dad and my grandma, who worked hard to see the Besseneckers break the cycle of poverty and lift themselves out of such dire straits.

Tractable poverty is like falling into a hole with some handholds, and most anyone reading this has had a family member escape this kind of poverty. Some great-grandpappy was born and raised in a shack and managed to break out of a life of dispossession. They were entrepreneurial. They saved their pennies. They worked hard. They invested wisely. They seized an opportunity. They got an education.

So if my dad and his family could find their way out of poverty, can't every poor family? Survival of the fittest, right? The hard-working and determined climb out, and the lazy and unmotivated remain poor.

> **The question of a person's economic class isn't about the laziness of the poor or the ingenuity of the rich.**

It's not that easy. There are a lot of hard-working, entrepreneurial penny savers who never seem to make it out of poverty and some self-absorbed, lazy rich people who never seem to make it into poverty. The question of a person's economic class isn't about the laziness of the poor or the ingenuity of the rich. Class and character are not always in a causal relationship. There is intractable poverty—a pernicious, death-grip kind of poverty that can trap a dozen generations of the same family without a hint of letting go, no matter how resourceful, ingenious and reliable they may be.

THE PUSH FORCES

There are outside "push" powers in this world, like massive economic engines working for the benefit of those in power, pressing families into poverty. The young men and women moving into slum communities as the hands and feet of Jesus need to understand the economic and infrastructural powers that create and maintain poverty if they hope to bring deliverance. It's the aggregate force of these things, along with forces discussed in the next chapter, that produce intractable poverty.

Economic pressure. Employment, wages, inflation, international sales, jobs that shift from one country to another—these are economic forces so often driven by multinational corporations, large-scale investment, the international banking industry or government deals. Decisions are made, deals are cut, production is outsourced, and the poorest laborers are at the mercy of others. Combined sales for the top two hundred corporations are more than the combined economies of all but ten countries on earth. That's a lot of money jumping across oceans at the command of precious few decision makers. While 27 percent of the world's sales go into the coffers of these top two hundred corporations, less than 1 percent of the world's workforce is employed by them.

A simple case in point: 70 percent of all bananas involved in international trade run through the accounts of just three companies: Chiquita, Dole and Del Monte. To help us understand the implications this has for the poor, let's look at the same situation in a different setting. Imagine, if you will, the enormous expanse of the Amazon jungle. Now imagine if only three monkeys controlled the distribution of the vast majority of all the bananas in the jungle. Even if the three monkeys were the most benevolent monkeys in the jungle, wouldn't it seem strange that millions of other jungle creatures would be forced to barter with only three monkeys in order to get their daily supply of bananas? What in the world would three monkeys do with the proceeds from the exchange of 70 percent of the Amazon's bananas? What else but buy up the all the coconuts? When wealth is concentrated it attracts the other wealth around it like a great magnet, and the more it attracts, the larger and stronger it becomes. Fewer and fewer people end up controlling more and more wealth. This kind of situation swirls far above the heads of the poor where they have no voice and little chance to influence. It's easy for them to get overlooked or, worse yet, used.

So long as there is poverty on the planet there will always be human beings willing to do just about anything for just about nothing. The latest global unemployment trends indicate that "of the over 2.8 billion workers in the world, nearly half still do not earn enough to lift themselves and their families above the US$2 a day poverty line." Let that reality sink in a bit. All day at a sewing machine or hauling bricks or rolling cigarettes or sorting garbage for a dollar or two. But what can you do if you live in a city where there is 30 percent unemployment? Workers making two dollars a day are better off than their neighbors who don't work at all. And so long as there is someone desperate enough to work for a dollar or two a day, there is someone else willing to exploit that labor for those of us who just want a cheap pair of jeans. The lower the labor wage, the more that can be made by someone who knows how to convert cheap labor into a profit. If you keep the bottom rung of laborers desperately poor there will always be dollar-per-day wage earners. It's to the advantage of those who own a controlling interest in labor-intensive companies to keep wages at their lowest possible level—a sort of twenty-first-century slavery with people working for less than they can live on with dignity yet enough on which to survive. Desperate people make for good gravel upon which those in power can build a highway to wealth. Poverty is the means by which some corporations are able to pull in extremely large profits and explains why so much work is outsourced to the developing world.

And workers who will do anything to keep from being unemployed are the reason incredible gaps exist between many CEOs and their lowest-wage employee. In his book *Saving the Corporate Soul* David Batstone describes the realities that affect blue-collar workers in America, workers like Robert Hemsley, a machinery operator for a paper mill in the state of Washington. The CEO for the mill makes 592 times more than Robert does. In 2001 Robert and his coworkers were threatened with layoffs because the mill wasn't making enough money, so they took a pay cut in order to help keep the company afloat. That same year the CEO received a $1.4 million stock bonus.

According to Batstone, business guru Peter Drucker was warning people about the dangers of the growing pay gap between CEOs and the average worker back in 1980. Those were the good old days when CEOs were making an average of "only" forty-six times more than rank-and-file employees. In companies like Robert's, a forty-six-fold difference in pay would be a welcome change for those laborers working hard to keep their CEO at near-emperor income levels. Taking into consideration the dollar-per-day wage of factory workers in the developing world where many garments for mega corporations like Wal-Mart or Disney are outsourced to, the disparity becomes even worse. These transnational corporations are tsunami-sized economies that roll in and out of poor areas, swallowing whole communities. In fact, of the one hundred largest economies on planet Earth, fifty are corporations.

> **Of the one hundred largest economies on planet Earth, fifty are corporations.**

Eighteen-year-old Mahamuda Akter was invited to tour the United States to speak on behalf of the Coalition for the Abolition of Sweatshops and Child Labor. As a sewing operator at a factory in Bangladesh, Mahamuda sews collars onto shirts fifteen hours a day for companies like Wal-Mart. "There is constant pressure on us to work faster. They beat us. They slap our faces. They use vulgar words. They make me cry," she says. The garment industry is notorious for perpetrating labor abuses—and giant retail chains often outsource to these kinds of factories. You may wonder how places like Wal-Mart can tolerate such pitifully low wages and blatant employee abuse. But for multinational corporate executives, Mahamuda's factory is one or two steps removed from them. When they send a bid out for one million T-shirts, they will snap up the contract offering to make shirts for one dollar each over another factory offering to make them for two dollars per shirt.

That's part of the reason we can buy clothes so cheaply at Wal-Mart and CEO H. Lee Scott can receive $29 million in total compensation for one year's worth of work. We can get cheap clothes and H. Lee Scott can get paid about $80,000 a day because Mahamuda and her coworkers are willing to work for so incredibly little.

Macroeconomic forces like this exert a great deal of pressure to keep a slave labor force operating. The power to hire and to fire, to lay-off and to promote, to close down and to build up is in the hands of a few. And if these few are primarily motivated by higher profits and if they possess the ability to increase their own share of the profits, then they will resist any force attempting to push labor wages up to livable levels. Without a board of directors that can sympathize with the lowest paid employee, there is no accountability to keep in check the human tendency to use power for personal gain. If executives act without conscience and are not willing to demand certain factory conditions before entertaining a contract from a factory, or if the corporation does not foster an environment that supports the company's decision makers in choosing higher production costs in order to reward factories with decent labor practices, the bid will always go to the sweatshop. Without a public that knows what's going on and that chooses to vote by means of our purchasing power, there is little to keep us all from plundering the poor simply by buying the items that save us the most money.

Pointing the finger is easy and even a little satisfying. Tolstoy said, "Everybody wants to change the world and nobody wants to change themselves." We are all susceptible to the temptation to increase our share in this world at the expense of those who don't have the same access to resources that we do—and it shows. Every time the gap between rich and poor is measured it is larger than the last time it was calculated. The World Bank claims that in the last forty years of the twentieth century, the gap in average income between the twenty richest countries and the twenty poorest countries doubled. Most people want a good economic foothold even if it's on the head of someone below them. So billions of dollars go skipping across oceans more or less unchecked, rewarding anyone who by any means can squeeze the most work out of a human being for the least pay.

Every time the gap between rich and poor is measured it is larger than the last time it was calculated.

The addiction to high profits represents one economic force that helps keep poverty alive and well on our planet. Those taking up the cause of the destitute will need to confront this form of oppression. But other economic forces, like international trade policies and powerful financial institutions, can also bend the rules in ways that curse the poor.

I was in Mexico City once when a large demonstration rolled through the Bellas Artes situated not far from the zocalo—a sort of gathering place for beggars, merchants, tourists and occasionally protesters. Farmers on tractors and on foot were waving signs and chanting slogans proclaiming their cause. Apparently, the American government had been helping failing U.S. farmers by buying up the surplus grain in the United States and then selling it for nearly nothing in Mexico, making it impossible for Mexican farmers to compete. Who would buy a bushel of corn from Tio Juan for twenty pesos when Uncle Sam is selling it for half that price? The practice, known as "dumping," may be saving American farmers from bankruptcy, but it is driving Mexican farmers into poverty. In the best light, those who use this policy are like a bull in a china shop: clumsy, short-sighted and so absorbed with self-interest that they ignore the potential impact their actions have on others. At worst the policy is cold-hearted exploitation. American farmers are not so much at fault; they too are facing economic forces intent on pushing them off family property in order to absorb their land into a corporate machine. But those behind the policy care more about exporting goods at any cost than about the farmers on either side of the border.

Today, agricultural subsidies seem to be getting addressed to some degree. The World Trade Organization meetings in Hong Kong in December

2005 were among the few that did not end in protests, yelling matches and walk-outs. However, international trade meetings almost always seem to end on a favorable note for rich countries. The Hong Kong meetings were no different. The few with the wealth hold disproportionate sway over the international trade game and will often use their influence without regard for those who cannot even hope to compete.

Whether it's the U.S. government brandishing its massive economy in ways that can be devastating to smaller, more precarious markets, or massive corporations searching for people desperate enough to work for the lowest possible wage, the poor so often are at the mercy of these economic powers. Those who would seek to befriend the poor must know how to speak into and influence the macroeconomic machine. Indeed there is little hope for the destitute worker unless some who are committed to the poor fight their way into the halls of power and become full-fledged decision makers who can affect billions of dollars internationally. Or, perhaps the new friars will inspire fresh conviction and resolve among current power holders so that they will face these forces with courage, ensuring that the poor are considered in their decisions.

Infrastructural forces. Poverty is not just the fault of the massive economic pressures driving the price of a human hour of labor to its lowest possible limits, or of governments using their power to bolster their flagging markets at the expense of others. Poverty is also fueled by political corruption and crumbling infrastructures. Police who participate in the underground markets of drugs and prostitution, judges who accept bribes, local officials wanting to reward friends and family members with government contracts, even the systems by which those of us in the middle class get loans, buy homes or access various services—these are some of the infrastructural forces that make the walls that surround the intractable poor too smooth to scale.

In his book *Good News About Injustice,* Gary Haugen tells numerous stories that reinforce the fact that local corruption contributes to the problem of poverty. Where rule of law has disintegrated, opportunists are given free reign. In India, for example, moneylenders known as *mudalali* are sometimes the only source of quick cash for those who are, practically speaking, shut out of the banking system. Haugen writes of Shama, a ten-year-old girl who had been working for two years to try to pay off a twenty-five-dollar debt. This is how it happened: The birth of her sister Mubarak had come with medical complications the family couldn't afford, so they sought the help of a mudalali. The mudalali agreed to give them the loan so long as the family was willing to offer Shama (then eight years old) as a laborer. Without access to a simple loan, this family had to choose between the life and health of one child and the bonded labor of another. Many families in similar economic circumstances have working children, so the decision was clear. Shama has to work for this moneylender in his cigarette manufacturing business. From 7:00 a.m. until 8:00 p.m. Shama sits on the floor closing the ends of cigarettes.

The local government does nothing to confront these moneylenders and can even benefit from the slave trade by collecting bribes from moneylenders in exchange for turning their eyes away. And so the profession thrives. The poor need access to quick cash, moneylenders need access to bonded labor, and the government needs the growth in their gross national product. That's how, according to the International Labor Organization, 186 million children aged five to seventeen can have their childhood sucked out of them through some of the worst forms of child labor.

There are many ways in which poor communities are innovative and truly thriving social colonies. Friendships can run deep and entrepreneurship can be extraordinary. But poverty, in its desperation, also creates infrastructures that are just as exploitative as the systems from the outside that grind the poor into the mud. Many slum communities are made up of "rich poor," "middle-class poor" and "poor poor." The "rich" and "middle-class" slum dwellers will sometimes take advantage of the poorest members of their community in order to get ahead—because those above them do the same thing. Many of the landlords in slum communities are poor themselves by Western standards. Almost everyone has someone below them on the socioeconomic ladder, and people don't have to be very far up the food chain to step on the head of those under them.

I can remember walking into the flat of a landlord in a garbage village (a community, usually in the developing world, that collects the trash of a city, bringing it into their streets and homes to sort and recycle). The stairwell to his apartment, if it could be called such, was the very same dark, garbage-strewn, rat-invested stairwell that the other tenants trudged up. However, when I entered his home, there were freshly painted walls, slick new tile floors and a large TV set. After my visit with him I continued up the dark corridor to hang out with the family that lived in the two-room hovel (with no bathroom) at the top. Their corrugated-tin roof was caving in, the father was suffering from a kidney disease and the mother from tuberculosis, and

Friends in the garbage village

two of the six children had been given away to agencies because the parents were too poor to care for them. Yet the landlord charged them excessive rent and this family paid it; there was no other option available for them and no government regulation helping to keep landlords like this one from charging unbearable rent prices. Righteous city infrastructures that are set up to keep communities running smoothly and to help protect the weak have collapsed, and makeshift systems that rake poor families deeper into poverty have taken their place.

Inaccessible systems. Not all forms of power are driven by corruption or greed. Some are simply the consequence of the systems that have been erected by people who know nothing about the challenges that poor people face in obtaining access to basic resources. The middle- and upper-class architects of various services build these systems with themselves in mind. Utilization of credit via the credit card, knowledge of the Internet, access to cheap transportation, the availability of a security deposit—these are the things the middle-class take for granted.

I remember planning a student conference on poverty in the Tenderloin district of San Francisco. There are ten thousand homeless people in this thirty-five-square-block area of the city. The population of the Tenderloin is three hundred times denser than in the rest of San Francisco. The streets are lined with porn theaters and residential motels. These motels are not only used by the prostitutes but also provide housing for those who might only be able to afford a week's rent. Part of our experience as the planning team was to spend the night in a residential motel. We stayed in the Aldrich Hotel on Jones Street. It was run by a friendly and industrious Indian family who did not own the building and likely worked for very little themselves. The hotel was somewhat of a shambles. Worn-through carpet, peeling paint, windows without screens and an old mattress on a creaking frame indicated that this was not like most of the hotels any of us had stayed in before. At least not in America.

I paid forty dollars for a fitful night of sleeping on a double bed with the guy who was my conference codirector. Street fights outside our window invaded our attempts at sleep. There was no private bathroom, no TV, no free toiletries (but it did have a little "waterfall" pouring from a crack in the ceiling just above the landing on the second floor). Still, with rent prices the way they are in the Bay area, this room was not too far out of line with the market rate for housing in the city. Since the unemployed often do not have the one-month's deposit necessary to move into an apartment, in the Tenderloin they live week to week in residential hotels like the Aldrich.

The next night I was going to stay with some friends, but that arrangement fell through. I decided that I should stay near the airport since I had an early flight the following morning. While our planning meeting proceeded I opened up my laptop, hooked up to the Internet via wireless connection in the home where the meeting was taking place and threw out a bid on Priceline.com. For forty-five dollars I stayed that night in the Marriott near the San Francisco airport. My room was immaculate; I had cable TV, a private bathroom full of free toiletries and two queen-sized beds all to myself. A newspaper was waiting outside my door at 4:30 a.m. when I left for the free hotel shuttle that whisked me off to the airport.

Much more energy is required for the homeless to access the systems by which I was able to book my room. Even with a local library's computer they often do not have the credit card number, home address, phone number and e-mail address that give the middle class and rich the ability to find and secure reasonably priced housing. What's more, the services created to help the poor tend to keep them concentrated in certain areas of town, which makes accessing the niceties of other areas of the city difficult. Such systems are not always created by wicked people who plot to make money off the poor or actively seek to lock them out of opportunity. Infrastructures like banking, housing and transportation are sometimes put in place by people who are simply out of touch with the realities of the poor and therefore create realities that make sense to them and the people they know—people who are almost always in the same social caste. The rich and middle class are heavily insulated; we end up building walls around our systems, making them easy to access for ourselves but harder to access for the poor.

THE WAY IT WAS SUPPOSED TO BE

Never have there been thousands of people dying because they are dangerously overfed sharing the planet with billions who are dying because they cannot get enough calories to sustain life. In the economic laws God established for the nation of Israel, there were built-in safety valves designed to keep the gap between rich and poor small. "There should be no poor among you," God says in Deuteronomy 15:4 (NIV). Every seven years, those who had loaned out money were to forgive any borrowers who had not been able to pay them back. Can you imagine the impact of such a law today? Credit card companies are founded on the hope that you will forever be paying on your debt but never paying it off. Such a law would limit the amount of borrowing that took place to the bare minimum, and insure that the rich had a vested interest in the poor getting back on their feet. In the agrarian life there were certain to be times when crops failed or disaster struck. The family of God was to loan freely to those in need. "If there is among you anyone in need, a member of your community in any of your towns within the land that the LORD your God is giving you, do not be hard-hearted or tight-fisted toward your needy neighbor. You should rather open your hand, willingly lending enough to meet the need, whatever it may be" (Deuteronomy 15:7-8). Loans given by any one person would likely have been small, since the lender would want to be certain that seven years of indebtedness would not pass before the borrower could pay it back; otherwise he or she would no longer be loaning the money but giving it away. The destiny of the borrower and lender were tied up together.

Even more radical was the Jubilee law. Every couple of generations (fifty years to be exact), all the land that one person had obtained from another person was to be returned. There would be no single family or clan who could take over the property of other families—at least not for very long. Who would want to accumulate a real-estate empire knowing it would eventually need to be returned?

Ancient Israel was to be a community working under the economic principle of solidarity. Rich and poor were bound together. If the poor could not get out of poverty, the rich would eventually be involved in seeing things righted. It would be a bizarre anomaly in Israel for a member of the community to get so indebted as to become an indentured servant. How strange an ancient Israelite would consider the great American pastime whereby a family gathers around a game board, and the objective of the game is to obtain all the property on the board, and then, after building houses and hotels, to charge your kin such exorbitant rent that each of them goes into financial ruin one by one. The Old Testament laws would not allow anyone to get rich out of interest income, real-estate development or usury . . . that is, if the Old Testament economic laws were actually followed. Unfortunately, the laws were not obeyed, at least not for long. Perhaps that is why the very same passage that states "There should be no poor among you" also says several verses later, "There will always be some in the land who are poor. That is why I am commanding you to share freely with the poor and with other Israelites in need" (Deuteronomy 15:11 NLT). Archaeologists have discovered that up until about 1000 B.C., personal dwellings in Israelite territory were essentially identical sizes. Beginning somewhere around the time of the kings, however, ruins reveal Palestinian towns with a few very large palatial homes, and many very small houses.

> **God's plan was to keep the gap between rich and poor small.**

It is clear from the Old Testament laws concerning capital, wealth and the treatment of the poor that God's plan was to keep the gap between rich and poor small. In his society there would be no H. Lee Scott making millions and Mahamuda Akter making almost nothing, since both have been equally created in his image. Both deserve the dignity of sufficiency. Neither family should suffer the intoxication of extreme wealth or the destitution of extreme poverty. Their destinies were meant to be bound up together.

In a world gone awry with islands of radical wealth in oceans of radical poverty, there is a tremendous need for those who can access the systems to insert themselves into poor communities—rich, young entrepreneurs who are willing to cast their lot with the poor and gain a vested interest in helping these communities find ways to correct the broken infrastructures and economies from inside the slums. We must welcome and encourage the handful of new friars who are asking to be set apart for just such an honor. But once inside the slum communities, their greatest challenge will be affecting the systems within them—the pull forces that keep the poor in intractable poverty.

SUCKED INTO POVERTY

Poverty sucks. That is to say, there are forces within poverty that pull families into a cycle of destitution and contribute to the intractability of the most desperate forms of poverty. They are the "pull forces" of poverty coming from within, such as the cultures and mindsets that exist among the poor, amounting to a kind of resignation to one's place in life. Or the repeatedly bad choices that many poor people make out of habit and brokenness and sin that compound their poverty. I also believe in active and intelligent forces of evil bent on trapping families in a state of impoverished despair. These are the cultural, personal and spiritual forces of poverty, and it is these powers that governments and international bodies like the UN have very little impact on. These things require people of faith to get close enough for long enough to have influence.

CULTURAL FORCES

There can grow up within a poor community a culture of "contentment" with the conditions that surround them. It's a form of resignation or fatalism. When you tire of trying to attain the unattainable you lose hope. That hopelessness feeds on itself, and soon you stop caring about yourself or your kids or the environment in which you're living. That's a pull force.

Father Ben Beltran is a Filipino Catholic priest who, since 1978, has lived among the garbage collectors of Smokey Mountain, a dumpsite in Manila, Philippines. As he became part of their community, many of his presuppositions about their motivations and values began to fall away. He saw how

Smokey Mountain

the area around their subculture shaped the way they thought and the way they reacted to things. These reactions were quite different from his way of thinking.

> The set of meanings and values that informed their way of life was different from mine. I soon discovered that I was a stranger in my own country. I was looking at the scavengers from the perspective of an outsider most of the time.

Perhaps what we as outsiders to garbage communities see as resignation or hopelessness is really a healthy dose of realism—a very practical view of the world.

> The people of Smokey Mountain believe in the basic inequality of each person. One is born into one's place in the scheme of things. . . . The denizens of the dumpsite do not resent the opulence of the rich because they think that is their own place and it is their fate to be rich. Their own destiny is to be scavengers—it is written in the palm of their hands and dictated by the

wheel of fortune. If times are good, they enjoy it. If times are bad, they endure it. They are on friendly terms with fate, and face any change in life with great calm and equanimity.

Poverty, at least in part, is perpetuated by "the way people look at themselves and the world, the stories they tell to make sense of their world." We are quick to judge the poor by our own perspective. Middle-class citizens often view the homeless poor as lazy because, we are told, anyone who works hard enough and saves can get ahead. But thinking only in the short term is natural in communities where tomorrow is so uncertain.

When things are tight in my household, we go out to eat less. We've found we can stretch our grocery dollars pretty far. It used to baffle us that friends who are just one step away from living on the street could go out to eat at fast-food restaurants every day when we feel it's such a rare treat. But when your housing is uncertain or nonexistent—making food storage and refrigeration tentative—fast food is logical even if it costs more money than preparing food yourself. And when you are in a situation where so much energy is consumed with getting through the day, the cost of shopping and cooking a meal goes beyond cash.

> **The more I connect myself to the poor,
> the more convinced I am that money is
> really the smaller part of the problem of poverty.**

The more I connect myself to the poor, the more convinced I am that money is really the smaller part of the problem of poverty. I am less quick to attribute laziness as the reason a person is poor or unemployed. Rather, it's about systems that surround the poor and cultures within their communities—cultures that make sense when you walk with people in them for a while, but whose values can sometimes increase the difficulty of escape. Believing that wealth can be built slowly over time is a huge leap for those in poor communities. Investment thinking and long-term planning run against the grain of a lifestyle so rooted in the present. "All the days of the poor are hard," Proverbs 15:15 says. Their future is so uncertain and the need in the present is so pressing. The overwhelming trouble of each day cultivates a culture whose gravitational force keeps the poor from saving and leveraging their capital for long-term benefit. The spending habits of the poor, which seem so undisciplined and foolish to the rich, make sense to them; the idea of saving for a goal that is so far away and doubtful seems foolish, like a waste of precious resources.

Unholy contentment. My family and a group of university students were coming to the end of our time living and serving in an Egyptian garbage community in Cairo. Living in this community for over a month had given us new eyes. What at first was repulsive—rotting garbage piled everywhere, animals feeding off the trash, mothers climbing rubbish mountains with their babies playing next to them in the refuse—was now quite normal. The hot, passionate desperation we felt regarding the conditions in the garbage village during the first few days had cooled to a settled comfortableness with life there. Was that OK? Maybe the life of a garbage collector wasn't all that bad. The people there seemed pretty content. The conditions were likely not much different from life in medieval Europe. Should we really be encouraging foreigners— especially rich, North American college students—to come into such places as agents of change and make themselves part of these slum communities?

I began to wrestle with God. This whole summer project seemed like a huge mistake. Calling students with notions of transformation to long-term residency in slum neighborhoods might only amount to bringing Western standards of housing and cleanliness to people who have developed their own culturally defined norms for quality of life and are just fine with how things are. "Oh God," I prayed, "If you want me to call students to lives of sacrifice and catalyzing change in the slums, then you'll have to convince me that it's the right thing to do. By the way," I added, "could you answer me in the next forty-eight hours, before we leave this place?" As soon as we got back to the States it would be my job to issue a call to students to leave their homes and move into places like the garbage village as servants to the poor.

Several hours later I had a dream. I dreamed about the dung truck. You could always smell the dung truck before seeing it. It was the kind of smell that was more like a taste at the back of your throat: pasty and bitter. The dung truck workers would pull alongside a building and haul out the animal waste that had accumulated on the ground level of the houses in the community as well as from the makeshift pens inside and outside people's homes. The community was known for raising pigs, but goats, chickens, donkeys and dogs were the most abundant creatures in the garbage village.

The men who served in this capacity would shovel dung into large wicker baskets and then—carrying the baskets on their shoulders or their heads—walk up a plank ramp to dump the contents into the back of a flat-bed truck. In the process they would become caked in dung from head to foot. Temperatures of over 100 degrees released the dung's pungent odor with a vengeance, making this task even more intense than can be appreciated by someone reading this in comfort.

In my dream I was walking past the dung truck. To my horror I saw my children, Hannah, Philip and Laura, sitting on top of the mountain of dung heaped on the bed of the truck. What struck me most about them was that they appeared perfectly content although every inch of their bodies was covered by animal waste. Then I felt the Lord speaking to me. He seemed to be saying, "As their father, are you satisfied? Even if they are satisfied, are you satisfied?"

> **A person's contentment with a situation of poverty does not make it OK.**

I am still sifting the impact of that dream, but the immediate implication was that a person's contentment with a situation of poverty does not make it OK. My passion for my kids is a shadowy reflection of God's heart, which yearns for his children to have more than the dung that surrounds them: not riches, but a life in which their needs are met in a way that doesn't mask their need for him. As Proverbs 30:8-9 says,

Give me neither poverty nor riches;
> feed me with the food that I need,
or I shall be full, and deny you,
> and say, "Who is the LORD?"

I came home and issued the call with passion. A fresh breed of friars lined the stage in the church where we conducted our debriefing, standing in commitment to go and make their homes among the poor.

The tendency toward resignation when times are hard or binging in times of abundance are cultural coping mechanisms that need to be brought into balance. Contentment and celebration are wonderful qualities in poor communities that often morph into a kind of "binge-purge" extreme, or a hand-to-mouth mentality, further entrenching their desperate position. New friars must look to incorporate healthy expressions of feasting and fasting into poor communities.

PERSONAL FORCES

Patrick lives on the streets of Madison, Wisconsin. He is a capable guy and has much of his health, but the realities of life for Patrick are harsh. Winters are cold and unforgiving, and he has sometimes shown up at our church with cuts and black eyes from being beat up on the street. One big reason why it's very hard for Patrick to land a job and keep an apartment is that he is an alcoholic. His habit of getting drunk daily has impoverished him materially and emotionally. What's more, he has turned down help to get sober more than once.

I think I could build a strong case that alcoholism and drug addiction all by themselves constitute forces keeping the poor poor. I am a little cautious to say every poor choice an addict makes to indulge his or her addiction is willful sin, because I don't fully understand where the disease overrides one's willpower. I have seen enough strong-willed addicts—with ironclad resolve to quit—fold under the unbearable pressure to give in to their addiction. But somewhere in the process of developing an addiction, a person must take responsibility for their bad choices.

To view the poor solely as victims does them a disservice. They are as frail and broken as the nonpoor. They make mistakes, and those mistakes compound their situation in exactly the same way that my sin and brokenness can make life harder for me. To give the poor the dignity of being human we must acknowledge that their poverty is, at least in part, entrenched by their own sin. Drugs, alcohol, dropping out of school, having children by multiple partners, quitting good jobs—these things can complicate and deepen poverty. Such actions are sometimes outgrowths of the despair that so often accompanies poverty, and people who have not lived the life of a hand-to-mouth marginalized person must be slow to point the finger. But bad choices are bad choices and still reap consequences no matter how reasonable these choices may seem given the internal and external forces that press a person toward them. Poverty has a way of magnifying the consequences of personal sin to a degree that the nonpoor don't experience.

Take for example two fifteen-year-olds producing a child out of wedlock. This happens every day in rich and poor communities alike. In both communities it is often one of the moms of the unwed couple or an extended family member who takes the lion's share of responsibility for raising the child. In the poor community the child competes for resources in a way that the child of the middle class and rich does not. The child of the poor will generally have less nutrition and a harder environment in which to study for school. Very often this kid will have inadequate health-care coverage and will likely move from one poor housing unit to another. Instability will become a part of life. The things that blocked access to resources for his or her parents will quickly become the things that prevent this child from overcoming poverty, so poverty is inherited and passed on just as wealth is. In addition, this child will put a strain on household assets in ways the richer child living with extended family will not. In middle-class and rich households, health care, food, decent housing and schooling are not issues for a child born out of wedlock. But for the poor, an unexpected child may mean someone else in the household will not get the medicine they need, because there isn't money left after the cost of the birth. An unwanted pregnancy and birth creates difficulty in any community. But the consequences among the poor are proportionally larger than they are among the rich. Sin is more expensive in poor communities.

Of course, every human—rich or poor—sins, and sin is costly for all of us. Augustine uses three analogies to describe sin: an inherited disease passed down from generation to generation, a power to which we are enslaved and a judgment pronounced for breaking a law. You and I are bent toward making bad choices that damage ourselves, our earth and our relationships with one another. *Sin* is the thoughts, words and actions that break things. We break ourselves, our loved ones, complete strangers and the earth with regularity. But the ultimate consequence of our tendency toward wrong, according to the Bible, is the shattering of our union with God.

Sin is more expensive in poor communities.

It was God's initiative to remedy sin at an unthinkable price: to enter the world in absolute vulnerability as the man Jesus, live perfectly and then accept upon himself the penalty for every act of evil. The historic crucifixion of Jesus Christ and the physical resurrection that followed were the crowning proof that our Creator had cleared a path for us. The way is called grace. God is both judge and savior. Anyone humble enough to acknowledge their need of his saving act gets the unearned prize of restoration, absolutely free of charge. No begging for forgiveness, no jumping through hoops, no purchase necessary. A simple "yes" to his offer, and fellowship between a holy God and a sin-stained human is forged anew—now with the promise of his Holy Spirit sent to comfort, empower and gift each believer. The person so good at breaking things now has the wherewithal to mend them.

So poor and rich alike sin, suffer under sin's bondage and are offered a way out of sin's power to cut us off from God. But when I say sin is more expensive in poor communities I mean that the net that softens the earthly consequences of our poor choices is often missing for the poor. They don't have access to the systems that support the nonpoor. And if despair has infected and destroyed the parent-child relationship (how can you care about your kids when you've stopped caring about yourself?), the social scaffolding that bears most of us when we stumble is unavailable as well.

That the poor sin should come as no surprise. Nor should the reality that their sin can compound their poverty. But this does not absolve us of our responsibility to care for the poor. Sin does not disqualify a person from receiving help. People receive help all the time despite the fact that they make bad choices. When we look at someone like Patrick whose life on the streets is so thoroughly connected to his alcoholism, we say he's only living the mess that he's chosen for himself. But what if the full effect of every one of our sins was pressed into our lives without the support structures of friends, family and access to loans or steady employment, which can so frequently reduce the impact of our sin? The poor are most certainly sinned against: by systemic injustice, by the tendency of the nonpoor to judge them or ignore them, by lack of access to the same systems that empower the rich and middle class. I only include the reality of their own sin as one of the forces that contributes to poverty because it cannot be ignored if we want to restore wholeness and dignity to those trapped in economic desperation. The new friars will be midwives

who help to bring renewal into the lives of those who have made mistakes but want to change.

Ryan spent the summer of 2003 in Manila, working with people who lived under a bridge, visiting prisoners and ministering in garbage communities. He recounts a story of how he learned to love a drunken man named Jomar. With his Filipino Christian friend Gerald he planned to go and cook a meal for Jomar and his family. They almost canceled due to a particularly destructive monsoon on that day.

Ryan (left) and friends

So we went up to Jomar's place and got totally soaked in the mean-time. I made pasta with pork/meat ragu and fresh Italian herb bread. I also brought him a Bible that I had bought that day because he told me when he was wasted drunk that he wanted one. We went into his very small squatter house and I took a seat on the inverted broken computer monitor that now serves as a chair. His mother, who is born again, and his family were there too. About 10 people total. . . . As we talked to Jomar (he speaks a little English, but not much) it didn't take long for the conversation to get serious. He said, "I want to get baptized, but I think I need to get sober first." I started to tell him that Jesus loves him so much and doesn't require us to be clean before we are able to come to him. He calls us to himself just as we are, and then gives us the power to change our sinful ways. We began speaking truth over him, including 1 John 1:9: "If we confess our sins, he is faithful and just and will forgive us our sins and cleanse us from all unrighteousness." His eyes started welling up with tears. We continued to speak the truth over him, with his whole family listening. After about 10 minutes of this he told Gerald that he wanted to accept Christ! I knelt on the gross floor in front of him, despite his resisting, and we prayed with him as he accepted Christ into his heart. He started weeping like a child midway through the prayer. While Jomar was crying out to God for forgiveness and change in Tagolog, his whole family (2 daughters, 2 sons, a wife and mother) were sitting by listening. After finishing the prayer, he got up hastily and ran over to his children to embrace them and ask for their forgiveness. He was still weeping.

I know from family experience that alcoholism does not always come under control with a profession of faith. Viv Grigg, the missionary to the slum communities of Manila, speaks of a Bible study that began from converted drunks. Viv confesses that every one of them died without seeing complete freedom from alcohol. However, the communities of men and women moving into slums with a commitment to love and to preach are building the kind of trust relationships that breathe life into the brokenness of the poor. They have an innate sense of what a holy life looks like but are sinful enough themselves to know not to preach from a pedestal but from the dirt. Calling the poor into dynamic relationships with their Creator is the first step to slaying the dragons of personal indulgence.

> **New friars preach not from a pedestal but from the dirt.**

SPIRITUAL FORCES

I once went to Skid Row in Los Angeles with a group of university students. We were approaching the end of a week-long conference that we were holding in a local church and had a lot of leftover food, so we decided to go to Skid Row to pass it out. We arrived at about 10:30 p.m., which gave us a view of the glamorous "City of Angels" that people don't often see. In those hours after dark but before the police push the homeless off the streets, little tents and big cardboard boxes line the concrete.

As our van pulled to a curb and we began to bring out the food, a line of about sixty people formed quietly and with order, as if queuing up for tickets to the theater. We had just enough food to go around. We dished up plate after plate of lukewarm pad thai, burritos, fried rice and chicken curry. Quite an eclectic dinner. Afterward the students and I fanned out to sit next to those we had served to spend a little time getting to know them. There was one man who did not eat. He was rail thin, had no shirt and was having a hard time getting his pants to stay on his nonexistent hips. He was looking up into the sky, swaying and speaking about foul acts, his face beaming. It seemed clear to me that there was something more than just substance abuse or mental illness at work. There was a darkness that I find hard to describe. I felt it in my spirit, and it made me shudder. He was tangled up in an evil delusion—a spiritual malevolence.

Other people in other places have seen this spiritual darkness among the poor. Father Simon, a Coptic priest who moved into a garbage community in Cairo, encountered a lawless jungle of cardboard homes suffering under a reign of terror. Jackie Pullinger began working in Hong Kong's "walled city," where even the police refused to go because it was ruled by people completely given over to wickedness. Viv Grigg encountered communities in the slums of Manila where evil was lord. Anyone doubting the reality of demonic forces active in poverty need only to have spent a night in these communities before Father Simon, Jackie Pullinger or Viv Grigg arrived. Each of them found deeply rooted spiritual forces that were not subject to community revitalization projects or microenterprise loan programs.

The apostle Peter likens the devil to a lion, prowling around looking for someone to devour (1 Peter 5:8), Jesus calls him "the prince of this world" (John 12:31 NIV), and Paul speaks of the devil as a spirit at work in the hearts of those who refuse to obey God (Ephesians 2:2). The Scriptures tell us he is able to trap people and hold them captive (2 Timothy 2:26). Greed, corruption, murder, oppression—these things are not only inherent in our nature but are fueled by a living being. Spiritual entities bent on crushing people do exist in slum communities and can only be vanquished by the power of Christ wielded by someone who knows him personally (see Acts 19:13-17). In Nigeria, for instance, exploitative shaman place curses on families and then claim that these curses can be forestalled only by giving a daughter over to the sex trade. Thousands of women are thus bound by a spiritual fear that will not be assuaged by municipal authorities or secular social workers. Whether you believe in the existence of personified evil or not, there are spiritually based activities in slum communities that entrench people's impoverished condition and cry out for a spiritual solution.

The existence of evil has confounded theologians and philosophers for centuries. Why would a God of love, who himself is the definition of goodness and righteousness and purity, tolerate the seeming free rein of wickedness? The short and best answer is, "I don't know." A slightly longer, yet still incomplete answer is that God values the mess of human freedom over the order of a puppet show. True freedom must include the freedom to embrace evil. God is not interested in "love slaves" whose affection is programmed but in free people who willingly choose him and follow his commands: do justice, love kindness and walk humbly with him (Micah 6:8).

God is not a distant impersonal force. We were made in his image, so like us he has personality and consciousness. Evil too has a persona and intelligence. Part of the reason poverty feels so intractable is because there is a conscious spiritual force committed to keeping people bound in states of oppression. Drug addiction, emotional resignation, greed, child prostitution,

Students who took up residence in a slum community for a summer

sweatshops—these are things dreamed up in hell, and they drive the feelings of despair that rule a slum. When you're desperate or even angry there is at least a shred of hope that things might be different, a holy discontent. But despair is what happens when you're tired of being desperate. And despair is a spiritual state that the enemy of God and humanity is actively and intelligently working to push each of us toward. Intractable poverty is a favorable environment to spread the despair illness. To ignore this need to confront spiritual forces by actively sowing a spirit of hope will short-circuit attempts to eliminate poverty.

ENOUGH!

Eliminating intractable poverty is not likely something that governments or the UN will accomplish. These powers can only affect the economic and perhaps the infrastructural portion of the equation. To really dig deeply into the wound of poverty will require thousands of healthy "blood cells" who will take on the entrenched viruses of culture, personal sin and spiritual forces: devoted, focused and radical men and women who are not afraid to link their destinies with the destinies of these poor communities, people who are willing to live with Jesus among the "least of these." And the "least of these" have never needed advocates more than they do now.

God's plan for humanity did not include poverty. His vision for the families of the earth was neither scarcity nor excess but sufficiency with his provision and guidance. Not wanting puppets, he gave us freedom to choose right from wrong; many of us have leaned into our inclination to hoard resources and exploit power. But God's heart is for solidarity alongside the oppressed, and it was this godly penchant of attachment to the powerless that infected people like David Von Stroh, Father Ben Beltran, Viv Grigg, Mother Teresa, St. Francis and St. Clare. God's penchant for throwing in his lot with the poor showed up in its purest form in first-century Palestine when the cries of another hungry mouth born into poverty pierced the ears of a young couple named Mary and Joseph.

4   THE VOLUNTARY POVERTY OF GOD

Unwed teenage pregnancy brings disgrace in any culture. But in the rural towns of the Middle East it is scandalous. Even more so when the girl claims her fiancé is not the father. In a village of four hundred families there is little chance for anonymity. Everybody knows everybody else's business as soon as it happens. Such a pregnancy brings reproach not only on the girl but on her father and brothers, whose job it is to ensure something like this doesn't happen. Even a righteous family would suffer the shame of such an event for a long time. Interesting, isn't it, that God would choose to come into this world via a peasant family, stirring up a cloud of shame by the way he entered? Jesus was considered the illegitimate son of a carpenter by every family in that village. Did he really have to show up on earth in a way that produced such dishonor?

JESUS, JUSTICE AND POVERTY

At the time of Jesus' birth there were a great many places of importance on the planet where he might have been born. In the first century, the city of Chang'an, China, was as near to a celestial city as any in the world. With half a million residents, it was likely the largest city on the face of the earth. Palaces and mansions surrounded beautifully ornate imperial gardens. What's more, the Chinese civilization was much further along technologically than any other civilization at that time:

> A many-sided genius named Zhang Heng devised the world's first seismograph in earthquake-prone China in AD 132. Salt miners, using iron drill bits

. . . drilled 4,800-foot-deep boreholes to extract salt from the earth. Miners also discovered natural gas in what they called "fire wells" and channeled it through pipes to outlets where it was used as fuel.

China would consistently beat the West by more than one thousand years in creating the devices that served to advance civilization. The imperial palace would have been quite a convenient place for God to show up in the first century, given that emperors were considered divine. What more obvious place could he have chosen if he wanted to instantly be acknowledged as Lord of Heaven?

That God chose the Hebrew people might be understandable given his commitment to Abraham and his promise to bless all the families of the earth through his offspring (Genesis 12:3). But if you're God and you're going to be born among the Hebrews, how about choosing the zenith of their political and religious life, say during David or Solomon's reign, or at least in the holy city, Jerusalem!

Or, if God must insist on being born during the age of the Roman Empire, why not be born among the Maccabees, who, 150 years before Christ, were so zealous for the law and the temple that they stirred up a religious and political revival? They were freedom-fighting martyrs during Jewish persecution under the tyrannical Antiochus Epiphanes. Or what about the Herods who were at least rich and powerful? And the location? Where in the Empire might God's appearance have made sense? Rome. Alexandria. Ephesus. Athens. There were Jews in many worthy cities of the Roman world. But Nazareth? In Galilee? That's tantamount to the president of the United States shutting down the White House, dismissing his staff and moving the Oval Office to a trailer park in Keokuk, Iowa, near the border of Missouri. People from Galilee were considered hicks. Those from Nazareth in Galilee were considered hicks by the hicks!

Why on earth would God choose to be born among a defeated people in a backwoods town under a shadow of dishonor through a dirt-poor, unwed teenager? Solidarity, that's why.

> **Why would God choose to be born among
> a defeated people in a backwoods town
> under a shadow of dishonor
> through a dirt-poor, unwed teenager?
> Solidarity, that's why.**

The very first statement Jesus ever voiced about his concern for poor, oppressed, marginalized people was when he cried out as one of them— eyes shut tight, mouth open wide, wailing, kicking, shaking and dripping with blood and amniotic fluid. It was one of the most profound acts of solidarity with the poor he could make. He cast his lot not with the world's emperors or with the rich and powerful but with the world's demoralized peasants. When God voted with his birth, he voted for the poor. It was the fulfillment of a long-awaited plan for God to live among the people he had made.

I WILL DWELL AMONG THEM

Throughout the Old Testament God kept insisting that he wanted to dwell in the midst of his people and their messy lives: "I will dwell among the Israelites, and I will be their God. And they shall know that I am the LORD their God, who brought them out of the land of Egypt that I might dwell among them" (Exodus 29:45-46). There's something about living with a group of people that changes the dynamic of a relationship. It is the key step in becoming incarnate.

TV is great. You can watch other people's problems from a distance and not have to get involved. Reality TV shows are especially engaging. Sometimes you can watch people's lives get seriously trashed as a form of entertainment, from the comfort of your living room. God could do that if he wanted. He could keep coolly distant from his creation and simply watch it all unfold without getting involved. But God is not a voyeur. He wants to be involved.

Heather Coaster, American missionary with Word Made Flesh, spent four months dwelling among the poor in Bolivia. She attached herself to the women whose intractable poverty has pushed them into the sex industry. When she came back to the United States, she did what she could to advocate for them. But there was something deeply unsatisfying about her attempts to help from a distance. She writes the following about her advocacy work.

Heather Coaster

It's such a convenient conversation. Sure, it strikes me. I read the staggering numbers, attach the unfathomable data to a story just to make it personal, and the somatic injustice rises up in my throat or turns in my stomach or threatens to keep me from sleep. There's a reminder again that things are not the way they're supposed to be, that all is not quite right. I am bothered by a sense somewhere between restlessness and calling. So I write essays and maybe even checks and I think about writing a letter to my Senator. I read the book or pick up the latest New York Times Magazine. Over a drink I discuss the theological, social and economic roots and implications. I pride myself in being aware. I appease my social conscience, thinking that my conversations and benefit dinners are all contributing to some global solution.

And maybe they are. God, I pray they are.

And I keep eating. I even end in dessert. I close the book, put a The End on the story, toss it all aside, pull the sheets back and climb into bed. There's not much more I can do, not tonight. And lucky for me, I don't have to. I have the unfathomable luxury of walking away, of signing off, of saying good night. While my conversations are coming to very neat, concise closes, she's tucking her kids in, putting her shoes on and taking the rest off. The red glow of her night is on and she's tossed from one set of dirty hands to another. There are rules in place, rules against going without protection, rules against sexual violence. But once her door is closed, the only rule is his desire. She only knows that tomorrow her kids will again be hungry, and this is the cost of her love for them. Yes, it matters today. It matters tonight, because there are still six hours until morning. And while we can afford those six hours, she cannot.

If all I have to offer her is conversation, awareness, words, then yes, I will give the rest of my life to the talk. But it's not. It can't be. It's not all I have and it's not enough.

Heather moved back to Bolivia long-term to become part of the community of dispossessed women whom she loves and for whose freedom she yearns. To minister from a distance was not enough. She wanted to become as Christ to these women. The emerging youth movement of which Heather is a part has radical notions of incarnation among the poor. To undertake an incarnational approach to ministry is to be sent as Jesus was sent—to empty yourself of all that alienates you from a people and to become to a significant degree as they are. Jesus told his followers, "As the Father has sent me, so I send you" (John 20:21). Even when Jesus sent his disciples out on a training mission he set them up incarnationally.

VOLUNTARY POVERTY AND THE FIRST MISSIONARIES

Jesus appointed twelve students who would be his apprentices, mostly uneducated working-class men, one activist-revolutionary and a man who made a small fortune by cheating others. No sooner had he granted them power to heal and confront demons than he sent them out in pairs as part of a training mission. They had had enough book learning and sermonizing; now it was time for them to discover for themselves what this "kingdom come" was all about. According to the biographer Mark, "[Jesus] told them to take nothing for their journey except a walking stick—no food, no traveler's bag, no money. He allowed them to wear sandals but not to take a change of clothes" (Mark 6:8-9 NLT). Their mission was threefold.

First, heal people. These might be the incurably sick or lame, people who couldn't see or walk or hear or who suffered wretched diseases and, as a result, would have been at the bottom of society, even if they were cared for by family. Their healing meant social restoration and release from a state of dependence.

Second, the disciples were to cast out demons. There were men and women, boys and girls plagued with what today might be diagnosed as destructive mental illnesses. They would cut themselves (Mark 5:5) or purposely burn themselves (Matthew 17:15) or speak with the identity of evil spirits (Luke 4:33-34). People in such a condition would have been shunned as outcasts. Some might have even been locked up (Mark 5:3). Their deliverance would have meant coming back into right relationship with themselves and with those they had alienated by their deviant behavior.

Finally, Jesus' students were to proclaim good news about the kingdom of God: "As you go, proclaim the good news, 'The kingdom of heaven has come near.' Cure the sick, raise the dead, cleanse the lepers, cast out demons. You received without payment; give without payment" (Matthew 10:7-8).

This was a mission trip without credit cards, without matching T-shirts, without suitcases, without portable water filtration systems, without traveler's checks. Those who followed Jesus would, at least for the purposes of this mission, take a vow of poverty and become dependent upon the people whom they were sent to serve. They were beggars of sorts. No selling bits of handkerchiefs they had blessed that contained healing power, no taking up special offerings at praise gatherings. They were simply to look for people who might show them hospitality and offer their homes as payment-in-kind for their preaching and healing. No money was to change hands. While the disciples were guests, even in the poorest home in town, they weren't to complain or move around if they didn't like the accommodations or food.

> **The kingdom of God had come near to the people because the disciples had come near to them.**

Remain in the same house, eating and drinking whatever they provide, for the laborer deserves to be paid. Do not move about from house to house. Whenever you enter a town and its people welcome you, eat what is set before you; cure the sick who are there, and say to them, "The kingdom of God has come near to you." (Luke 10:7-9)

There would be no hotels or restaurants for the disciples, no running from event to event in air-conditioned buses. The students of Jesus were to draw close to people, enter their lives—actually touch their leprous bodies, eat what they ate, stay in their homes and become part of the household. The kingdom of God had come near to the people because the disciples had come near to them.

That was the vehicle for the transmission of the kingdom of God. It was a spiritual microbe contracted by close contact with Jesus freaks in places as intimate and personal as people's homes. But to properly pass it on, the disciples needed to strip themselves of the insulating power of money, food and extra clothes. Their profound neediness was a gift, a gift that would force them to depend on the Father whom Jesus talked about and upon the generosity of the townspeople to whom Jesus was sending them. Granted, first-century Mediterranean society valued hospitality, even to perfect strangers, by providing food and shelter. Still, a person would not venture on a journey without the items that Jesus ordered the disciples to leave behind. Voluntary poverty was the best way Jesus knew to move his followers into the arms of God and bind them to the needy people who would welcome them. The same thing has been true for his followers throughout the ages right up to today. That's why Heather left her comfortable home to live among and serve the poor of Bolivia, and that's also what motivated a rich, young Italian playboy to tie himself to the poor seven hundred years ago.

FROM RICHES TO VOLUNTARY POVERTY

Giovanni Bernardone (Francesco to his friends) was about twenty-six when he started the Franciscans in the early part of the thirteenth century. He didn't start out attempting to found the order that would become the longest continuous stream of Christian youth intent on placing themselves among the poorest people on earth. In fact Francesco was really a pretty riotous young man without much interest in the poor. An early biographer writing shortly after Francis's death said that Francis was brought up "indulgently and carelessly . . . [and was] taught shameful and detestable things full of excess and lewdness. . . . He boiled in the sins of youthful heat." Like so many since who have left all to serve Jesus among the poor, Francis started out filthy rich and lived like it.

Despite his life of luxury, his practice of carousing with friends and his fetish for accumulating fine clothing (his father was a textile merchant), Francis was bored with life by the age of twenty. In November of 1202 the chance for chivalry, knighthood and playing with explosives or boiling oil— the dream of every rich bored young man at the time—came. Provincial wrangling between the merchant class, to which Francis's family belonged, and the nobility came to blows. The war essentially consisted of one battle, which was a disaster for Francis and his rich friends from Assisi. Francis survived but was taken captive. Languishing for a year in a dank prison, Francis's health took a beating. Donald Spotto, in his remarkable biography *Re-*

luctant Saint, calls medieval prisons "a disease incubator." In fact, the malaria Francis contracted while waiting for terms of release to be negotiated probably hastened his early death twenty-four years later. Malaria was a recurring nightmare for him. However, Francis lived through the initial ordeal and returned to Assisi a shadow of the man who left.

Francis's recovery was slow and his depression deepened. Somehow defeat and prison had taken all the fun out of drunken debauchery. But early in 1205 another opportunity to redeem his military "career" emerged. A nobleman answering Pope Innocent III's call for the Fourth Crusade invited young Francis to join him. Here was his shot at nobility. Before departing for the adventure, Francis had a dream. In it, he was led into a chamber where he looked upon all the armor, weapons and trimmings of a knight. Certain that this was an omen foretelling his heroism, Francis left Assisi boasting that he would one day be a great prince. However, just a day into his trip his malaria flared up. In a feverish delirium, Francis heard a voice asking him where he was going. He said he intended to earn his knighthood in battle. But the voice simply asked him whether the master or the servant was the better one to follow, and then insisted that Francis was listening just to the servant. He was instructed in this mysterious exchange to return to Assisi and await further orders. Francis departed for home, arriving once again as a failure.

Francis of Assisi, by Gary Nauman

After his recovery, and having given up hope of receiving a sign, Francis returned one day from an errand of his father's in a neighboring town. Taking some rest in the shade of San Damiano, a chapel decaying from neglect, Francis stopped to look at the image of the crucified Christ. A voice "tender and kind" spoke to him: "Francis, don't you see that my house is being destroyed? Go then and rebuild it for me." This was what he had waited for. Better than carousing, better than killing, better than being the local fashion king, Francis had received a word from God.

If Francis had wanted to begin an agency at that point he might have dubbed it "Habitat for Divinity." But collecting followers was the furthest thing from his mind. Filled with a sense of purpose, Francis rushed off and began the work of rebuilding San Damiano, apparently taking this word from God at face value. He became compulsive about reconstructing San Damiano. Selling his father's goods to generate some cash for the broken-down chapel rendered Francis a lunatic—or at least extremely eccentric. He became an acute embarrassment to his family, so his father publicly beat him in order to save face and help persuade him to come to his senses. It didn't help. Unmoved in his mission, Francis was finally locked up in a storage room for two weeks until his father went away on business. His sympathetic mother set him free from his "house arrest," and Francis essentially ran away from home. He found himself frightened, cold and hungry, his only shelter a dark cave just outside town—hardly a pious beginning to his mission from God.

A final showdown with his father brought him out of his cave for a public trial before Assisi's bishop, Guido. At the trial, Francis formally broke all ties with his family and paid his father back for the clothes he had pawned for money to help with the reconstruction of San Damiano. The rumors of Francis's insanity were not helped when he stripped himself of every stitch of clothing he had on and handed it all over to the bishop along with a bag of money. Public nudity, voices in the midst of delirium and estrangement from family—it's almost as great a beginning to ministry as the shame of teenage pregnancy and alleged angelic visitation.

After more than two years of labor, Francis had made substantial progress on the restoration of three chapels—San Damiano, San Pietro della Spina and Santa Maria della Porziuncula. By that time he had begun caring for lepers, but nothing quite like the Franciscans that we know and love had emerged. Then in February of 1208 something happened that would change the nature of Francis's work.

Since Francis had restored Santa Maria as a functioning church, services could once more be performed from its altar. It was the first sermon in this now operational church that I believe changed the direction of Francis's ministry. The priest that morning read the account of sending the disciples with the instruction to "take nothing for your journey, no staff, nor bag, nor bread, nor money—not even an extra tunic" (Luke 9:3). The voluntary poverty of the first followers of Jesus created some sort of seismic activity in Francis's soul—especially considering the extreme wealth enjoyed by many of the clergy in the thirteenth century. Though he was by no means wealthy now that he had "divorced" his family, Francis did have an extra tunic, a walking stick, sandals and a belt. Inspired by Jesus' words, Francis turned these items over to the priest at Santa Maria and soon added the ministry of preaching to his mission.

This move to preaching seems to have changed the nature of what Francis was about. It was the vehicle by which many would come to be infected by Francis's spirit of self-sacrifice and his abandoned service to the poor, and join him in his mission. Beginning in 1208, others responded to Francis's uncomplicated preaching by asking to follow him. He had no desire to lead others, but neither did he want to stand in the way of those who wanted to work alongside him. One of his first companions was another son of a wealthy merchant, Bernard Quintavalle. On hearing Francis's simple sermon, Bernard invited him to his palatial home so they could talk in more detail. Joined by a friend of Bernard's named Peter, they spoke well into the night about the material-free life. The thought of living simply, helping the sick and answering the call of Christ to rebuild his church was compelling to Bernard and Peter, who wondered if this could be God's call for them too. Seeking the confirmation of Scripture on the matter the next morning, the three young men went to church and opened randomly to three different gospel passages—a common practice in pre-Enlightenment times. The first passage was Jesus' charge to the rich, young ruler, "Go, sell what you own, and give the money to the poor, and you will have treasure in heaven; then come, follow me" (Mark 10:21). The second was Christ's instructions to the disciples to take nothing for their journey—the same passage that recently had so moved Francis. The third was Jesus' description of the cost of discipleship: "If any want to become my followers, let them deny themselves and take up their cross daily and follow me" (Luke 9:23). That sealed it for the two new recruits. Francis was now part of a society whether he sought it or not. Within a year of that event there were about a dozen idealists camping out together and taking Jesus' words in the Gospels quite literally.

POOR CLARE

Just a few years after the start of Francis's order, on March 18, 1212, the seeds of another order germinated, this time in a young woman. On that brisk Italian night eighteen-year-old Clare Offreduccio snuck out of her Assisian home for a clandestine meeting. This was not a rebellious teenager stealing away under cover of dark in order to engage in some kind of silly prank or passionate interlude with a young man. On that destiny-forging Palm Sunday evening, Francis wed Clare to Jesus Christ and to a life of voluntary poverty.

The preaching of Francis was a magnet for idealists regardless of gender. Thomas of Celano, the first biographer for Francis, describes Clare as "young in age, mature in spirit, steadfast in purpose and most eager in her desire for di-

St. Clare, by Janine Bessenecker

vine love, endowed with wisdom and excelling in humility, bright in name, more brilliant in life, most brilliant in character." For years the beautiful but fiercely independent Clare had spurned the machinations of her very wealthy family to marry her off. There were certainly rich and handsome suitors who would have gladly solved the family problem of Clare's single-ness. To be a wealthy fifteen-year-old girl and unwed was strange in Clare's day; to be eighteen and single was a downright embarrassment, making it appear that something was wrong with her or the family. And her younger sisters wouldn't be able to marry unless Clare did so first. Rumors spread and the pressure to marry increased.

On that Sunday evening when Clare knelt to pledge herself to the Fran-ciscan ideal, Francis cut her hair, shaving the crown of her head (a practice of the monastic orders that perhaps harkens back to the Nazirite vow), and then covered her head with a veil. Dressed in sackcloth, she was whisked away to a Benedictine nunnery, as it would have been out of the question for her to live with the dozen or so brothers holed up with Francis. The next day the family patriarchs, learning of Clare's folly, raided the Benedictine house to "rescue" Clare from her impulsive decision and delusion under the teachings of a madman. But Clare was neither impulsive nor deluded. She pulled off her veil, revealing the tonsure cut into her hair, and claimed the refuge the church afforded those who would make such a pledge.

The excitement of a family kidnap attempt was not the Benedictine sis-ters' cup of tea. They asked Francis to do something else with Clare besides foist her and the unwanted attention that came with her onto their com-munity. Since the brothers were now living at Saint Mary's, Francis moved Clare into an addition he had made to San Damiano, and she spent the next forty-one years living as austerely as the brothers. She opened the floodgates for young women and was soon joined by her fifteen-year-old sister, Catherine, and eventually by her own widowed mother. Although Clare was expected to live the single life in keeping with medieval norms that associated celibacy with the clergy, she held the conviction that fol-lowing Jesus is sweeter than yielding to the social pressure to marry at all costs. Writing to Agnes of Prague, daughter to the king of Bohemia, Clare addresses Agnes's decision to refuse marriage to Emperor Frederick II and join the Poor Clares: "You, more than others, could have enjoyed the magnificence and honor and dignity of the world, and could have been married to the illustrious Emperor with splendor befitting you and His Excellency. You have rejected these things and have chosen with your whole heart and soul a life of holy poverty and destitution. Thus, you took a spouse of a more noble lineage."

Within twenty-five years Clare drew fifty other women to the Franciscan life, and just hours before her death she received papal approval for the rule she had written for her community, thereby becoming the first woman to define a rule of life for a community of women. Many men, bishops and popes included, tried to dissuade Clare from the strict rule of absolute poverty that governed the lives of the sisters, but she stubbornly refused to live in any other way. If poverty was good enough for the Son of God, it was good enough for them.

The two movements of the Franciscans and the Poor Clares grew up side by side, each order asking those who joined to pledge themselves to a life of poverty. Francis, unfortunately, did not die soon enough to avoid seeing his order torn from its ideals. He was reluctant to write a rule for the order. He would have been glad for the leaders within the movement to simply require the brothers to devote themselves to singing and preaching, to working with their hands and to living in voluntary poverty. But some leaders, along with Pope Innocent III, deemed Francis's harsh lifestyle as "too severe for human flesh and blood." Others tried to push the movement toward scholasticism. This was devastating for Francis near the end of his life. He feared that a devotion to study would distract the brothers from their devotion to prayer, to a life of poverty (Francis liked to say he and the brothers were wed to Lady Poverty), and to simple preaching. In one letter to Pietro Staccia, the provincial minister of the Franciscans in Bologna and founder of a Franciscan house of studies, Francis wrote, "You are trying to destroy my order; it is my desire and will that my brethren, following the example of Jesus Christ, shall give more time to prayer than to study."

As the order experienced inevitable growing pains, and debates arose about whether the brothers should work or beg, Francis wrote his last testament chronicling the beginnings of the order and laying out some of his final wishes.

> And very happily we stayed in poor and abandoned churches, and we were ignorant and subject to all men. And I worked with my hands and still wish to work; and it is my firm will that all the other brethren should do some manual labor which belongs to an honest way of life. . . . And if we should not be given reward for our labor, let us have recourse to the bounty of the Lord and beg our bread from door to door.

Quite simply Francis wanted his followers to avoid those things that might draw them away from the simple life of preaching and praying and caring for the poor, voluntarily becoming poor themselves so as to stand alongside the dispossessed and diseased. He wanted to imitate Jesus as best he knew how by following Jesus' commands to the letter. Jesus was God in a human shell with all its frailties and pains and vulnerabilities. If Jesus could embrace the human condition, then Francis (along with Clare and any who sought to follow them) should be compelled to embrace the condition of the least and the lost. The apostle Paul describes the early leaders of the church in a way that is fitting also of Francis, Clare and their friends, "as poor, yet making many rich; as having nothing, and yet possessing everything" (2 Corinthians 6:10).

THE HIDDEN BURDEN

Looking at the life of someone like Francis or Clare who became disentangled from the chains of wealth has drawing power. And in a society that has gone mad with materialism, there is something refreshing about simplicity. With the quest for money and things comes a hidden burden, barely noticeable at first but excruciatingly heavy by the time you recognize that you are trapped by your wealth.

On our tenth wedding anniversary Janine and I received two plane tickets as a gift, so we decided to visit the U.S. city of St. Francis—San Francisco. We walked more that weekend than I can remember ever walking in one weekend before. San Francisco is famous for its reputation as a destination for tourists and panhandlers. Consequently, we encountered people begging

> **Possessions can be a hindrance;**
> **giving them away can grant new freedom.**

at what seemed like every corner. Not content to pass by but not comfortable handing out cash either (we didn't have that much anyway), we decided to buy bags of fruit and give out apples, oranges and bananas with a word of blessing or a greeting. It was a small thing, but it was what we could do in such a short visit as tourists to an unfamiliar city. When we started out, traipsing up those often-photographed steep hills lined with row houses, the fruit felt like a great encumbrance. But as we had the privilege of handing it out, our load got lighter and lighter. It seemed like a parable to us. Possessions can be a hindrance; giving them away can grant new freedom.

Francis's and Clare's life illustrate this, serving as a picture of just how attractive downward mobility can be to the middle class and rich. They embraced Christ's example and chose a life of poverty. Jesus had promised that the coming kingdom would be good news to the poor. The Franciscans and Clares would embody that reality. They wanted to enflesh this gospel to those at the very bottom of the rubbish heap by stripping themselves of all worldly riches and seeking the endowment of spiritual wealth in its place. They would become real to the poor by becoming poor themselves, imitating Christ who voluntarily chose physical poverty and "moved into the neighborhood" (John 1:14 *The Message*), entering into the lives of people. They would achieve a kind of incarnation.

INCARNATIONAL

Pursuing Jesus' Descent into Humanity

Faye Yu lives in Freetown, Sierra Leone, in the postwar horror of a punishing ten-year civil conflict. Word Made Flesh has planted a small team there in order to incarnate the good news of Christ among the children who were conscripted into that terrible war. As the war heated up in the 1990s, rule of law dissolved and a rampage without any moral check ensued. Ten thousand children in this small country were forced into the war, some as young as five years old. If they refused to kill on behalf of any number of "revolutionary armies" battling for control of the country, limbs were cut off. Sierra Leone now has a disproportionate number of amputees. One child recounts, "Before I was captured, the rebels shot my father and mother in front of me, and having killed them, one of the commandos grabbed me by the throat, tied both of my hands, cut parts of my body with a blade and placed cocaine in it. I had no option but to join them because I no longer had parents." After the children were brainwashed and drugged they were often put on the frontlines of battle. Some were even forced to "wash" their families by killing their own relatives. Similar numbers of little kids forced to fight were also abducted into sexual slavery and hard labor. Rape of girls was organized and widespread. Many became sex toys for older men. Even younger boys were coerced to rape. "We do not even want to tell about these crimes. Many of us who lived through that horror cannot bear to talk about it. We don't want to remember. It is too terrible for you to imagine. Even we cannot imagine how these things happened to us."

It is in the wake of this robbery of childhood and destruction of right and wrong that Faye and her team work to restore a semblance of normality to

Faye Yu, center

the children—some kind of permission to be children. They run a program they call Lighthouse, helping to tutor kids in their schoolwork, read to them, play games and worship with them. On Saturdays the missionaries run another club for about three hundred children. The home Faye shares with another Word Made Flesh missionary, Cami, is sometimes full of these young visitors who come to hang out. Kids hungry for proper adult attention swarm them. Ones suffering malaria may stay the night. Mostly they share meals and play at Faye and Cami's place, calling them "mother." "They are so adorable," Faye says, "and all of them want to hug you and hold your hand. They watch all that you do and want to imitate it. These past few weeks I have been doing the chicken dance and other funky interpretive dance/gestures from the front for the kids to imitate so as to keep them distracted and engaged. Two hundred unengaged kids can be a loud, chaotic situation. I must admit, I am tired of the chicken dance, especially since when I walk down the street in Freetown I run into kids who greet me with the chicken dance."

What new friars like Faye and Cami and old friars like Francis and Clare excel at is breaking out of the padding that separates and protects us from the harsh realities of poverty by embracing it voluntarily and stepping into relationship with the poor without the power dynamic that is normally present between the poor and nonpoor. When the poor see "outsiders" like Faye subject to the very same conditions and realities under which they are suffering, something very powerful emerges in the nature of the relationship. Faye becomes a sister and a mother in ways that would be difficult if she drove into their neighborhoods to do ministry but lived a more comfortable life elsewhere.

Incarnation is not easy.

But incarnation is not easy. For Faye, the glamour of a life of service among the poor, if there is such a thing, was short-lived. Her early journals betray a period of testing and complaining. Being constantly dirty, having legs peppered with bug bites, the heat, the difficulty of life without modern conveniences—all of this wears on a person. Living in a context where cruelty perpetrated against children is continually uncovered means depression is close at hand. And at twenty-eight, Faye worries about being single. Living among and serving the poor sometimes feels like a curse to a single woman. "It sucks," she writes. "I have chosen a life that is radical (but not really radical if you look at the saints throughout church history)—that freaks out many of the men I come across. I overwhelm them."

But living incarnationally also gives perspective, helping us to see others, God and ourselves in new ways. Faye shares, "The probability of meeting a guy who will have the same passion for transformation, will not be overwhelmed by who I am and will choose to journey with me down this path is not high, but then we worship a God who is outside of probability. I do trust that God wants to give me the best and a full, beautiful life, and if that means singleness (which I and my extended family are praying it is not), I want what he has chosen for me and not what I think is best." Choosing a life among an oppressed community brings with it a kind of purifying power. "My selfishness and things that make me ugly are brought out to the surface," Faye says, "and God is making me into a more beautiful person."

Incarnating the gospel in difficult places does not just benefit the needy. When Jesus sent his disciples out with "no staff, nor bag, nor bread, nor money—not even an extra tunic" (Luke 9:3), it was also to their profit. They were weaned from their addiction to self-protection and comfort, and they learned to live trusting a God who could multiply loaves. Someone could even argue that the *disciples* were the mission field that Jesus was focused on when he sent them out penniless.

THE GLOBAL URBAN TREK

In 1999, while I was engaged in a master's program in international development, I began praying about how I might become invested in a movement to incarnate the gospel among the poor, like the Franciscans had done. I wondered what such a movement would look like in the twenty-first century. It was about that time that I first learned about Viv Grigg. A young New Zealander who had moved to the Philippines, he was a picture of the modern-day Franciscan to me, and I was captivated by his example. In his twenties he was working as a missionary at a Bible school in Manila, helping to establish a middle-class church. But Viv was possessed by a kind of emptiness—a soulful unrest. "My life was unfulfilled," he writes in a biographical work called *Companion to the Poor.* "The philosopher within me found no answers to the search for meaning; the artist found no fulfillment in the search for perfection and ultimate truth; the leader had not found the center of destiny and purpose towards which to lead others. All three voices told me I still was far from the place of God's call."

Then he was invited to the home of one of his students, Mario, whose family lived on a pineapple plantation on the island of Mindanao. The seven thousand workers for the pineapple factory lived in slum communities on the land that they once had owned. Now a transnational corporation paid them a barely livable wage while their work generated millions of dollars in canned pineapple sales that mostly stayed in the pockets of a few people in America. Mario's house was made of items he had scavenged from a dump. His parents both worked the maximum amount of time allowed by the plantation (four hours per day) but could not afford medicine for a skin disease from which his father suffered.

After a week in Mario's home, Viv returned to Manila more disturbed than ever. He began to hunt for a slum community into which he could weave the thread of his own life by moving there. At first he was misunderstood, and many concerned friends and missionaries tried to talk him out of his radical notions of stepping into the world of the poor. Still he persisted. At one point in his journey of faith in the slum communities, Viv climbed a one-hundred-foot mountain of stinking, rotting garbage and walked through the community of ten thousand men, women and children who lived and worked at the dump. Weeping, he cried out to God to do something about the plight of the desperately poor. God spoke into the brokenness of Viv's heart that he had sent his Son into the stench of human poverty and now was calling others to follow his example. Viv took God at his word and began to invite others into the incarnational life of serving the poorest of the poor. Reading Viv's story planted a seed for me that would germinate later that year.

In the fall of 1999, as director for InterVarsity's short-term mission programs, I began to dream about what it might be like to set up experiences for students to live and learn in slum communities during their summer break. Perhaps God was calling others like Viv to leave their middle-class lives behind and bind themselves to the urban poor. The idea possessed me. I lost so much sleep in those first few months as I began thinking and planning how I might call students to listen for the voice of God calling them to take up residence in slum communities.

Because I had worked for InterVarsity for more than a dozen years, I had some trust built up with our accounting department. I asked if they would set up an account for something I would call the Global Urban Trek. Having little idea how I would pay for it, I called some staff friends from around the country in September of 2000 to come to the U.S. Center for World Missions in Pasadena, California, to dream with me about how we might get students to hear God's call to the poorest of the poor by leading them into slum communities. I began charging things to that account—planning meetings, advance trips to places like Cairo, Egypt, and Kolkata, India (formerly Calcutta). We planned to travel to six megacities in order to find ministries that could put our students in slum communities. There were students to recruit, brochures to produce, a website to build. It was all very energizing. We were like Peter, stepping over the side of a boat in order to meet Jesus out on the water. I felt certain he had called us to stand out on the sea with him.

Before long the wind and the waves started to scare me. Staff who had earlier believed in the vision of the Global Urban Trek began to back out. From fourteen staff initially committed to pulling off the experiment, we were whittled down to seven. Those who remained were the youngest and least-experienced staff. Some of the set-up trips met with disappointment and skepticism. Nationals and missionaries on the field were reluctant to place American college students in slum communities. Few of the ministries seemed to understand what we were trying to do. Some discouraged us from attempting such a foolhardy plan, saying it was too dangerous. Criticisms and questions seemed to come from every corner. I was beginning to sink.

That fall of 2000 I was at a retreat with a number of missions-minded InterVarsity staff. The supervisor for one of the staff whom I was expecting to lead a Trek team was there. She told me that this person was pulling out of the program because it seemed like the Trek was beginning to fall apart. In many ways they were right. Most of my initial notions of how to carry this out had been rearranged, and I was beginning to despair. Why not cut my losses, find a way to pay back what I had spent, and drop the whole idea? "God," I prayed, "if you want me to continue down this path, you're going to need to convince me to keep going. Would you please speak to me by the end of the day, because each day we delay dropping this thing it gets more expensive?"

The twenty-minute drive home from the retreat site was enough time to have an encounter with the crucified Christ. The transaction was so profound I can picture in my mind's eye exactly where I was on Highway 51 when he spoke to me. He told me three things quite clearly. First, "The ups and downs of your emotions are no basis for determining my will in this matter." Second, "Don't you know that intractable poverty is evil? Don't you believe I want to deliver people from such conditions?" Finally, he directed my mind to a passage we had studied that day at the retreat. It was the passage on the sending of the disciples without money or an extra tunic that was preached about in the chapel of Santa Maria and that so compelled Francis. Jesus told his followers that when they entered the homes where they were sent, they should "cure the sick who are there, and say to them, 'The kingdom of God has come near to you'" (Luke 10:9). On that drive home God spoke to me and said that the reason his kingdom had come near was because his disciples had entered into people's homes and realities. For the kingdom of God to come near to slum communities, kingdom people need to become part of the slum-dweller's household.

> **For the kingdom of God to come near to slum communities, kingdom people need to become part of the slum-dweller's household.**

That short drive home has done more than nearly anything else to sustain me in the process of asking students to consider God's call to make their homes among the poor. I pushed ahead and eventually found eighty students willing to take up the challenge to live in slum communities for the summer of 2001. We conducted orientation in Los Angeles and then fanned out to Mexico City, Manila, Kolkata, Cairo, Nairobi and Bangkok.

I asked Viv to come from New Zealand to our debriefing time in L.A. at the end of the summer, when all eighty students would be back together after having lived and worked in slum communities. I was going to give them the opportunity to stand in response to God's call to serve the poorest of the poor, and I wanted Viv there to lay hands on them and bless them. Honestly, I had no idea if anyone would stand to such a sobering call. Viv spoke to the students on just how costly his life in the slums had been. His health had been compromised, he had married quite late in life, and many other opportunities had

Viv Grigg

passed him by. "Those of you going to live in the slums in Calcutta will need to build teams of twice the size you desire because half of you will return within six months," he told them. Not exactly the "rah-rah" inspiration for students to rise up and "claim their blessing."

On that final morning of debriefing, I asked for students to stand if they felt that God had called them to the poor for at least two years. Viv and I both wept as thirty students stood in response to the call. One by one we went to them, anointed them with oil and prayed over them. Today, some of those standing have embraced poverty as an incarnational lifestyle choice in order to reach those trapped in intractable poverty.

POVERTY'S SISTERS

One of those students was David Von Stroh, the Bangkok slum-dweller whom we met at the beginning of the book. He has learned that incarnation is a choice he must make every day. Options for nice clothing, nice housing and food are easily available. He identifies with Paige Young, an instructor in the Servant Partners training school, who confessed that when she first moved into a slum community of North Africa she thought she had made some kind of final and conclusive decision to incarnate the gospel among the poor. What she discovered was that she needed to embrace the incarnation on a continual basis. Inspired, David writes:

I thought like Paige, that back at some point in the past, whether a quiet time of prayer in Boston, or a call session at a Trek debriefing, I had surrendered to the call and decided on a life of incarnation. But that was just the first step. Each day, incarnation is a choice. I'm always tempted with easier ways out—compromises, or healthy moderations, depending on how you look at it. It would be a lot easier to have just been able to decide on incarnation and then follow in autopilot. But my journey with Jesus is that much richer when I have to daily live out and reaffirm this decision to incarnate with free will. It makes ministry not just about accomplishment or objectives, but a discovery.

It's the little choices to live simply and share day-to-day life with his slum community neighbors that give David rapport. Walking alongside the rickety boardwalks over sewage each day with his neighbors, eating where they eat, sleeping where they sleep, hanging out where they hang out—all of these allow a kind of companionship not available to those outside the community.

One of David's friends, Kak, collects bits of garbage to recycle or resell. Kak has struggled with alcohol as long as David has known him and suffers deep depression. His wife and children left him, and Kak has threatened to hang himself. David has often stumbled upon Kak passed out on the walkways of the slum neighborhood. Once, David saw Kak preparing to sniff some paint thinner. David came up to him, tossed the paint thinner out and tore up the rag Kak was getting ready to sniff. Kak listened as David told him of God's love and of his own concern for him—how grieved he was to see Kak destroying himself by abusing his body. Later, as David and some other believers in the community were meeting and singing hymns, Kak came and sat at the back of the room. David walked to the back and sat next to him.

David's incarnate lifestyle had earned him the right to confront Kak and still maintain a friendship.

A FATHER'S BLESSING

Faye, Viv, David, Francis and Clare pursued their calling at some cost. Although Clare won over her family, there is no indication that Francis did. The new friars will also face the excruciating struggle of trying to describe a lifestyle that appears radical and foolish to family members in order to receive their blessing if not their wholehearted support.

The Global Urban Trek gives me the immense privilege of offering those in their late teens and early twenties a father's blessing. I will often ask those who have not experienced the unreserved support of their parents to serve the poor to stand so that I might bless them. As a dad I have often prayed over my children that God would grant them the honor of being a servant to the poorest of the poor. The Trek gives me a chance to extend that blessing to those who are ten years or so older than my children. I'm not sure why, but I am always moved to tears when so many stand or come forward to be blessed by a dad who would be delighted to see his kids care for people who are trapped in poverty. Maybe it's because so many of them begin sobbing as I pray to express my gratitude to God over the choice they have made. What an incredible struggle for a child to seek to honor parents and yet obey a call of God that involves a move toward poverty.

I have certainly struggled with how to advise people in college who sense a call to follow Christ among the marginalized when their parents are adamantly opposed. Indeed, parents, even those who don't profess to believe in Jesus, are gifts from God. We are adjured to respect them. I was told once by the father of a young woman on a Trek that he would hold me personally responsible if any harm befell his daughter. It shook me up. His voice was raised and he threatened legal action if anything happened. Another young woman came up to me recently during Trek orientation and told me that her father had forbidden her to make any sort of commitment to serve the poor vocationally. She felt greatly conflicted because she sensed God calling her to empty herself on behalf of the poor. Not being so bold as Francis by offering to shave the tonsure on her head, nor wanting to provoke a kidnap attempt, I suggested that even if she chose not to make a public confession of service to the poor at the end of the Trek in honor of her father, that Jesus would be quite capable of sorting out her dual desire to honor her dad and, at the same time, obey God.

The twenties are a hard time in regard to navigating the parent-child relationship. The resistance and rebellion of teenage years have passed, a healthy respect for one's parents is beginning to grow, and yet the need to define a course of life (perhaps very different than one's parents) emerges. With patience and respect, most manage to win their parents over, helping them to accept a trajectory for their lives that will lead them into slum communities rather than into status, suburban comfort and financial security. But those seeking to identify with the poor in order to serve them and bring them news of Christ's love will need to figure out how to respond to family and friends who, in genuine concern, attempt to discourage them from the voluntary hardship that comes with ministry on the margins. Some will call the new friars to the more socially acceptable ascendancy to a higher class. Faye says her non-Christian friends "want me to be safe and happy—they love that I am helping the poor but wish I could do it without the radical simplicity/suffering bit."

But with a compulsion to incarnate the gospel among the bottom of the human food chain comes also a quest for devotion and spirituality that is hard to achieve in a life of material overabundance. Following Christ in his example of downward mobility brings a kind of intimacy and identification with the Savior that can be experienced in few other ways.

I had dinner with Jesus earlier this year. He sleeps on the streets around Santa Monica pier and goes by the name Bill.

Heidi Williams, the coordinator for InterVarsity's summer mission programs, was leading a meeting of Global Urban Trek directors in L.A. in April of 2005. She charged each of us to take a homeless person to dinner and get to know their story. We were attempting to understand the five forces of intractable poverty. So we divided up and headed out to pray and extend a hand of friendship to those who live out on the streets, just around the corner from the student hostel in which we were meeting. I prayed, "Jesus, I'd really like to have dinner with you tonight. Would you grace me with your presence?"

A few of us ended up at a McDonald's where many homeless hang out. While we were waiting for our order, a man with longish hair and a beard, wearing ragged clothes, stepped up next to me. He had such weathered skin it was clear he'd been living outside. "I'll just have cup of water," he told the person behind the counter. *Hmm,* I thought, *this guy sort of looks like Jesus.*

"Would you like to have more than that?" I asked him. Bill sat down with us and told his story of schizophrenia and homelessness. "You know, I'm sort of like Jesus," he said, and then went on to quote Jesus from Matthew 8:20, "'The foxes had holes but the Son of Man had no place to rest his head.'"

"You *are* kind of like Jesus," I agreed.

"I know I'm not *really* Jesus," he confessed. "I'm not that far gone yet."

Jesus was in fact homeless during his ministry years. He made his disciples homeless when he sent them out to announce the kingdom. There is some kind of strange connection between those at the bottom of society and Jesus—more than simply the fact that Jesus chose to live as one who was poor. Jesus is present in society's dregs, mysteriously "there" in the form of the least of the world.

As we tried to locate city services in the area that might give "Jesus of Santa Monica" a place to sleep and maybe a program to deal with his schizophrenia, it became abundantly clear just how hard it is to address the issues that keep some people locked in a cycle of desperation. Bill had gotten so cold and tired of sleeping outside that he stole a meal at a restaurant just to get a few nights in a prison bed. Now he has a police record, and the next time he tries that, he'll face a three-year sentence, which is probably more "prison bed" than he would like.

Somebody in a uniform gave us directions to the Santa Monica shelter. The directions were incorrect by one block, so we wandered around looking for the building, which really set Bill off. "They're all like that!" he said with anger. "They lie. Everyone lies to me." That kind of thinking has served to alienate him from his family and others who try to help. He imagines people are intentionally deceiving him, so he puts up walls, making it harder to receive help. Mental illness and our inability to effectively deal with diseases like schizophrenia are huge reasons why so many are stuck living on the street.

We finally stumbled onto Captain Ida of the nearby Salvation Army. Bill banged on the window of the agency, shouting, "Hey, I'm not Jesus," which frightened the old women studying the Bible in a room that looked out onto the street. At first the captain shooed him away; after all, he wasn't Jesus and they were closed. Then she saw Heidi and me with him, and we looked normal enough. Coming outside, she graciously offered to set up an appointment for the next day with Mr. Brown, who would assess Bill's situation. And she thought there might be an opening on Thursday in the shelter. Mr. Brown could possibly refer Bill to a program that would get him a bed and help for his schizophrenia.

Slum communities are kinds of chapels in which one can meet face to face with Christ in the dispossessed.

I hope Bill followed through and kept the appointment, though I will likely never know. But that experience was a devotional moment for me; it was an act of communion with God. The apostolic orders of people living among the poor are motivated, in part, by the ways in which they encounter Jesus in people like Bill. Slum communities are kinds of chapels in which one can meet face to face with Christ in the dispossessed.

DAMNED GOATS

Perhaps the most disturbing picture Jesus ever painted about the underclass is located in Matthew 25. Jesus was in the middle of a set of sermon illustrations designed to answer a question about the end of the world. Beginning in verse 31 he describes what the day of judgment will be like through an allegory. In this story, like so many others in the Bible, the righteous are rewarded and the wicked are damned. But the basis for their destiny is not related to some kind of verbal profession of faith, for both sheep and goats call him "Lord." Rather their destiny is determined by their treatment of people in need. Perhaps this is the truest barometer of genuine faith; any parrot can be taught to say "Lord," but acting out a belief in a God who cares for the "least" and who rewards his followers for serving them is the real test of faith.

At the end of the age, the Son of Man will be like a shepherd at shearing time or in the evening, when sheep and goats need to be separated. They live together in the field because they eat more or less the same thing. But they face different destinies when it comes time to shear them or to pen them at night. They have to be separated. It will be the same with people at the end of time as we know it. The Son of Man will divide people into two camps. One group, the sheep, will "inherit the kingdom" and enter into a place of rest with Jesus; the other group, the goats, will be sent out from the company of God's Son and become company for the devil instead.

What determined these radically different destinations? The goat-people didn't give Jesus any food when he was starving, didn't visit him when he was in prison (among other things), while the sheep-people did. The punch line of the parable is the absolute surprise of both groups when Jesus announces their destinies because of how they treated him. "When on earth did we see you in such a needy state?" they both ask after picking their jaws up off the floor. "Just as you did not do it to one of the least of these," he tells the damned goats, "you did not do it to me." The sheep inherit the kingdom because they gave Jesus food and drink when he was in need and visited him when he was sick and in prison. They also welcomed him into their homes when he was on the streets of Santa Monica and gave him something to wear when his clothes were so ragged that they barely covered him. All that they had provided for "the least" they had actually provided to Jesus unawares. And when the goats closed their hearts and kept their fists tightly closed to those who had desperate needs, they were unwittingly turning their backs on the one who could determine their eternal fate. At the end of time the mask of the needy will be lifted, and to all of our surprise, Jesus will be found underneath.

There is some legitimate question as to whether Jesus was in fact referring to his disciples and not to random outcasts when he spoke of "the least of these." Talking to the sheep he says, "Truly I tell you, just as you did it to one of the least of these *who are members of my family,* you did it to me" (Matthew 25:40, italics mine). After all, Jesus had just finished telling about the terrible things his followers will suffer at the end of the age: torture, death and hatred, to name just a few (Matthew 24:9). "The least"

> **We often seek the "worthy" poor, those who are spotless saints and complete victims.**

may mean those in a state of need not because they were born into the margins like so many of the poor, but because they were being persecuted for following Jesus. Either way, the goats are still damned because they did not meet the needs of people who were suffering, whether students of Jesus or those who were needy simply because the forces of poverty had driven them into a state of desperation.

It's not always easy to tell right off why someone is hungry or homeless, nor does it fit with the whole of Jesus' teaching to suggest we should first determine whether someone is in need because they follow him so that we can withhold help from those who don't know Jesus. We often seek the "worthy" poor, those who are spotless saints and complete victims. And until we find that person, we walk by the "unworthy" poor and think, *You've got yourself into that mess so you can get yourself out.* I'm just glad God doesn't put the yardstick next to me that I sometimes put next to others before deciding whether I'll help. On the contrary, Jesus taught us to extend help not just to those who are good to us but even to our enemies and oppressors—people with serious issues. Maybe that's why our response to the needy is such an accurate measure of our faith. We ultimately extend to others the sort of grace we have experienced through Christ.

However you work the theological math in this parable, Jesus radically identifies with the underclass. He ties their identity together with his own. Callousness or kindness to people at the bottom is callousness or kindness to him. Proverbs 19:17 says, "Whoever is kind to the poor lends to the LORD, / and will be repaid in full." And Mother Teresa said that in the poor we find Jesus in a distressing disguise. This truth is central to many of the servants of Christ who walk among the poor. In serving the poor, they find a level of devotion and intimacy with Christ that is hard to obtain in any other way. And sometimes the most profound way to serve the poor is simply to walk alongside them.

THE MINISTRY OF SITTING AROUND

Ngaatendwe (or Gati for short) was part of a family considered the ruling elite of Zimbabwe. She moved to the United States with her family at the age of nine. I first met Gati in the summer of 2001 when, as a college student, she was accepted into the Global Urban Trek. She was an intelligent journalism major who wanted to live and serve among the urban poor in Cairo, Egypt, for a summer. I was so impressed with the combination of brilliance and compassion she demonstrated that summer that when my wife and I took a team to Cairo the next year we asked her to come along as staff. Tensions that year between the U.S. State Department and the government of

Gati

Zimbabwe meant that she would likely not be able to get back into the States upon our return from Cairo. This was problematic, as she had another year of school at Sacramento State University in California. With incredible disapointment, Gati sent us off while she remained behind to pray for the Trek. Near the middle of the summer the team received a letter from Gati. It was just the word we needed to hear at just the right time. We had been living and working in one of Cairo's garbage communities. Heat, sickness and a general sense of ineffectiveness had been rattling us, making us wonder if we were really of any use. Gati's words gave us fresh perspective: "Enter into the ministry of sitting around," she encouraged us. Take time to sit with the garbage collectors. Sip tea. Smoke a hookah (the water pipes stationed at every corner tea shop that seemed so central to Egyptian socialization). Gati urged us to enter into the reality of the people by releasing ourselves from the compulsion to *do* in order to take time to *be*.

She was right. The gift we came to bring was the gift of coming near. Not just coming near physically to teach English or work in the local clinic, but coming near emotionally to grow attached to people and learn to love. To love individuals in the garbage community was to love Christ and to love Christ was to love the people who had welcomed us into their neighborhood. That was without question the most profound summer in the life of our family. Something soulful happened that summer when we entered into communion with Christ in the people of that community.

In the summer of 2005, Gati's home country of Zimbabwe was embroiled in a campaign they called "Drive Out the Rubbish." Thousands of families were forcibly evicted from Harare's slums and moved to rural areas in a clean-up campaign that left a wake of human destruction. That same summer Gati—the daughter of Zimbabwean privilege—relocated herself into a slum community of Mexico City. She joined Servant Partners, and though she could easily live the life of a diplomat's child, she has chosen to live out a quest for holiness by drawing near to the urban poor and sharing in their harsh reality. Like the other new friars, Gati is experiencing the privilege of serving Christ by serving the "least," and in the process, becoming more like him.

DRINKING IN THE GRIEF WITH JESUS

Before Heidi Williams served as coordinator for InterVarsity's summer mission programs she was part of a team in Kolkata, India. There she im-

Heidi Williams, right

mersed herself in the realities of intractable poverty and served in Mother Teresa's Home for the Destitute and Dying. In that place of hardship and suffering she began to see what Mother Teresa had seen: the person of Jesus bound up somehow with the poor. She decided to draw near to him in the clothing of human desperation. She took a good long drink of the grief of Jesus over the suffering of people trapped in poverty and touched Christ in the process.

Well, I had my first major breakdown of the trip. Yesterday I went to the House for the Dying in Kalighat (Kalighat is not only the temple, but the entire area surrounding it). . . . At first it wasn't so bad. I started out washing the rubber sheets that cover the women's beds. It was easy and monotonous, and kept me from having to actually interact with any of the women, so even though it was kind of a gross job, I didn't really mind. But even that was a little intense. Whenever I looked up, there were the rows of skeletal women, just sitting or laying in their beds, waiting to be bathed or fed or have the sheets changed, all of them waiting to die. And then there were no more sheets, and I had to help another volunteer get a bedpan under one of the women. Her entire body was all curled up. She couldn't straighten out her legs and every movement hurt her so that she moaned. She has been there, in the House for the Dying, for 25 years!

How does that happen, that you would be "dying" for so long? After being there for so long she spoke pretty good English and knew exactly how things were supposed to happen, so she bossily directed us in the proper way to arrange her nightie and place the "napkin" (diaper) and the bedpan, but every time we had to touch her it caused such pain. I was so afraid that I would hurt her even more—the women there all look like they weigh about 50 pounds; they are nothing but skin and bones. It's terrible to look at someone's legs and see that the knee is the biggest part—like the legs of a stick person with big circles drawn where knees would be, that is what these women's legs looked like. With each touch I was sure bones were just going to snap under my fingers, they seemed so, so fragile.

I spent a lot of time massaging and oiling bodies, rubbing the tough, leathery skin and feeling every bump of every bone, because there was no fat or muscle in between. It was horrible. I was just overwhelmed by grief, but while I was there I mostly managed to keep it in, except when Shad and I were on the roof hanging laundry I did cry a little. I didn't want to start freaking out there, though, and shoved all the sadness and loneliness and despair and anger and frustration and confusion—just put all of it away. But it's not something I could get rid of for long. Those at home, they can't understand if they haven't seen it.

How did things get so bad? How did these women get so bad and no one took care of them before this? Where are their families and friends? It feels so lonely. I'm afraid they think no one loves them, and I wanted so much for them to know that I love them and that Jesus loves them, but I didn't know what to do. I sat next to one woman and just massaged her head and sang to her for 45 minutes. She was so young, not more than 25, and so beautiful, and it was so hard at that moment to believe that God is good and that he is there, but I sang worship songs of love and freedom, and prayed that even though she didn't understand most of the words, she would somehow feel what I was saying to her.

But then after I left, I still didn't have any time to process. It took us forever to get back home. . . . At first I was just sniffling and had a few tears, but then Joel asked me how I was doing and I lost it. We came out to the little alcove and I just sobbed, wailed. It was some of the most intense grief of my entire life.

But the beautiful thing is that as I was letting go of all that sorrow, and knowing that what I feel is only a tiny fraction of what Jesus feels, he began to show me joyful things too, how much joy it brings him when we take care of the dying and love them in his name. How happy it makes him when we receive those in need. When they brought a dying man into the House, a sister next to me said, "Here comes Jesus" and I thought that was the most amazing thing I have ever heard. I want so much to see it that way. But I just wish that there was not the need for the House in the first place. But until Jesus comes back (and every day I pray more and more that it will be soon) one of the most joyful things we can do is receive him in the people around us.

Like Bill in Santa Monica, like those living as scavengers in dump sites, and like the men and women in the House of the Dying in Kolkata, Jesus waits for us to draw near to him. It is so much easier to pass by. But what joy will be ours at the end of time when the costume is pulled aside and we see Jesus in that drunk we helped or in the street kid we reached out to. And as Gati advised, sometimes it is enough simply to sit with someone who is suffering. From time to time, we may even have the honor of sharing in their suffering.

THE FELLOWSHIP OF SHARING IN HIS SUFFERING

There is something about voluntarily suffering alongside the voiceless that connects us with Christ in a way that few other things can. The apostle Paul cries out, "I want to know Christ and the power of his resurrection and the sharing of his sufferings by becoming like him in his death" (Philippians 3:10). The new friars understand this. Their move to a slum community is, in part, an act of worship. Some are ready to suffer and to die to themselves as a form of devotion. All of them, however, will be confronted with suffering and will be faced with the choice of entering into the pain.

Walter and Adriana Forcatto work with poor street kids through Word Made Flesh. In Lima, Peru, they bound themselves to a community of street children who were often harangued by the police. Once, Walter came upon two street kids being chased by an officer. When the police officer caught up with them, he began beating one of the boys. The twelve-year-old boy began crying. Walter ran up to intervene, explaining that he was a street educator and could help since he knew these kids. The officer brushed him off and began to take the children to his police car. When backup police came, the officer sent one of his comrades to inform Walter that he was interfering with police business. "Why do you help animals and trash like street children and why are you trying to help them escape?" an officer demanded. Walter ended up being dragged to the police station with the two boys, with the officers hurling insults at them as they drove. When they arrived at the station, the police pulled the street kids out of the car by their hair. One officer began physically abusing one of the boys with his nightstick, uttering profanities at the boy and calling him an animal. When the child began going into convulsions and the officer contin-

Walter and Adriana Forcatto with daughter Cora

ued to beat him, Walter could stand by no longer. He demanded that the officer stop beating the boy, calling him an abusive animal. That was enough to turn the officer's fury from the boy onto Walter. Knowing he could not lay a hand on the American foreigner, the police tried to demoralize Walter in other ways by searching him and interrogating him.

Later, thinking it was not at all a reaction Christ would have had, Walter reflected on his outburst toward the police officer. "I am faced with the depth of my own brokenness when I look at Jesus and see the power and love he demonstrated in his words and actions in front of the accusations of his torturers and killers. . . . Can I bear to not only have my life taken away, but to actually lay it down on my own initiative? And if I can't what does this say about my Christian faith?" As Walter identified with the suffering of the street children and stepped into their pain and abuse, he discovered places of brokenness and self-righteousness in his life that needed to be held up to the light of Christ. The kind of discovery Walter made came only because he chose to submerge himself in the lives of the street kids he loved. "If, 'in his suffering and abandonment on the cross, Jesus became the brother of the suffering and abandoned,'" reflects Walter on a quotation from theologian Jürgen Moltmann, "then our service to the poor and oppressed implies a sweet act of love to God." In sharing in the sufferings of the children on the streets of Lima, Walter enjoyed a union with Christ and a form of devotion that is changing him more radically into the image of Jesus.

The apostle Peter wrote, "But rejoice insofar as you are sharing Christ's sufferings, so that you may also be glad and shout for joy when his glory is

> **The new friars are really quite ordinary.**
> **They are not the elite branch of the church;**
> **they are broken men and women on a journey.**

revealed" (1 Peter 4:13). Intimacy with Christ means sharing in his sufferings, which becomes a doorway into deeper devotion because it involves dying to yourself—something that is so important to the emerging order of new friars.

I know Gati, Heidi, Walter and Adriana. Some of the new friars I know quite well. They have lived in my home and worked alongside me. For those of you feeling like you could never be so noble, radical and spiritual, let me assure you that they are made of flesh and blood and carry in them the same tendencies to mess up as you or I do. In my experience, the new friars are really quite ordinary. They are not the elite branch of the church—the Christian Marines or the Navy Seals of the faith. They are broken men and women on a journey. They experience fear, loneliness and anger. They suffer pride, lust and hatred. In some ways, that is why some of them have made the choice to live among the poor. Moving into a slum community is not so much an attempt to be "good" but is rather a place where God can better shape them on the potter's wheel of service. The new friars are not perfect, but one thing many of them are intent on is pursuing Christ. This is the heart of their true mission.

NAMING CHRIST IN ORDER THAT CHRIST MAY NAME ME

From the time I first began following Jesus, I wanted to be a missionary. Early on in our life of faith Janine and I took the Perspectives on the World Christian Movement course: an extensive examination of the history of Christian expansion and the modern missionary movement. I was like a mouse in a cheese factory. I ate up everything in sight. The course emphasized work among those groups of people who might have no chance of hearing the amazing truths about Jesus without someone from the outside coming to tell them. I soon quit my job at a furniture store in order for Janine and me to visit a friend in Mexico City who was working with Latin American Mission. When we returned, I decided that I wanted to work with students through InterVarsity Christian Fellowship.

One of the first things I did in my work with InterVarsity was to take students overseas to explore missions as a career. Janine and I led groups of students to Eastern Europe in the summers of 1988 and 1989 before the fall of the Berlin Wall. We worked with refugees in the former Yugoslavia and helped brothers and sisters in Hungary with youth ministry as we worked together on building an orphanage. We also met clandestinely with Romanian pastors who had suffered enormously under the cruel dictatorial regime of Nicolae Ceausescu, in order to deliver relief supplies to them and share together some words of encouragement. It was life-giving and invigorating to be on the field if only for a short time.

In 1990 Janine and I began applying to mission organizations that would place us overseas more permanently. Ultimately, though, we decided that the organizations were not good matches with our particular needs and gifts, and we continued working at InterVarsity. When my boss pulled the plug on Janine and me taking a group of students to serve Palestinian refugees, however, I became deeply discouraged. It was January in Wisconsin, which was reason enough to get depressed for those who don't care for darkness or cold weather. I very distinctly remember shoveling snow from our driveway wondering what had come of all my great expectations to be a missionary in the most challenging environment on earth. Now I was a homeowner in my late twenties with one child. The fact that I even had a driveway was disheartening, let alone the realization that precious time and energy had to go into hauling snow from it one shovelful at a time only for it to get covered again in a few days.

I had read earlier that day the passage in Matthew where Jesus gives Simon the name Peter or "Rocky": "You are Peter, and on this rock I will build my church." Jesus gave Peter a name that defined his mission for the rest of his life. He gave Peter an identity. That's what I wanted him to do for me—to give me an identity that would help define my specific mission and calling. "Oh God," I cried, "I wish you would name me!"

Then the Lord spoke quite clearly to a deep place within my spirit: "Peter named me first," he said. At first I was a bit taken aback. Then I recognized that in this passage, the naming of Peter was prompted only because Peter had just answered Jesus' question, "Who do you say that I am?" Peter had replied, "You are the Messiah, the Son of the living God" (Matthew 16:16). Apparently I had not yet fully understood Jesus' identity and acknowledged his Messiahship.

As I puzzled, clarification came with a few more shovelfuls of snow and another statement coming from somewhere outside of me yet not audible. "You love my mission more than you love me," Jesus said to me. At first I found this a bit offensive. I suppose Peter might have felt the same way when Jesus kept asking him later, "Do you love me?" (John 21:15-17). *How can this be,* I wondered? *Of course I love you, Lord.* But then I began to ask myself, what was it that motivated me? What was it that I thought about and dreamed about and obsessed about? It was his mission. Indeed, I did love his mission more than I loved him. It was true. I was in pursuit of Christ's mission, and in the process I had passed by the Mission Giver without so much as a "hello."

As wonderful as it is to bring the kingdom of God to the hollow places on earth, even this is rubbish in comparison to the surpassing greatness of knowing Christ Jesus. Intimacy with Christ must be first. Without it, mission is empty and self-serving. I stopped pursuing his mission on that day and began giving myself more completely to him—whether that would lead me permanently overseas or not. New friars will need to learn how the quest for Christ must have supremacy in their lives. If they can do that, they just may be able to save civilization.

BARBARIC FRIARS

The Celts are a great example of how God can use and change imperfect people when they are intent on pursuing him. Before being Christianized the Celts were a truly terrifying people. They apparently loved to collect the heads of their enemies, proudly displaying them "in their temples and on their palisades; they even hung them from their belts as ornaments, used them as footballs in victory celebrations and were fond of employing skull tops as ceremonial drinking bowls." From descriptions they sound as if they were drunk with violence. Painted blue and running buck-naked at their opponents, swinging objects specially designed to maim, they would strike fear into the heart of the bravest Roman soldier. The Romans were so frightened when they first encountered the Celtic warriors that they would flee "whole and unhurt, almost before they had seen their untried foe, without any attempt to fight or even to give back the battle-shout. None were slain while actually fighting; they were cut down from behind whilst hindering one another's flight in a confused struggling mass."

Surprisingly, however, this barbaric tribe gave the world some of the first preaching orders four hundred years after the death of the original disciples.

And like so many of the missionary monks and nuns of the past, devotion to Jesus was at the core of their efforts.

It all started with the capture of a sixteen-year-old boy during an invasion by one of these fearsome Celtic hordes. Young Patrick was living quite comfortably in what was then referred to as Britannia. England was a frontier land in those days, and the people who lived there were subject to a good old-fashioned slave raid now and again by the barbarians who lived near the edges of the Empire. Wealthy families like Patrick's were especially at risk. The Celtic band that swooped down on Patrick's home car-

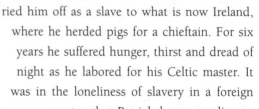

ried him off as a slave to what is now Ireland, where he herded pigs for a chieftain. For six years he suffered hunger, thirst and dread of night as he labored for his Celtic master. It was in the loneliness of slavery in a foreign country that Patrick began to cling to the Christian faith of his childhood and started hearing the voice God. At twenty-two he was guided by God's messages to a ship some two hundred miles from his place of servitude. Patrick eventually found himself back home in the safety of

St. Patrick, by Gary Nauman

his parent's arms, but not for long. A vision of a man from Ireland came to him, bearing letters that begged him to return. So young Friar Patrick embarked on a lengthy period of education and ordination before returning to Ireland as a missionary bishop.

On the eve of Patrick's ordination, weighed down by his conscience, he confessed to a friend a sin he committed when he was about fifteen (it may have been murder). Later on his "friend" spilled the dirt on Patrick to those in "civilized" Britain who resented his ministry in Ireland to the uncouth Celtic savages. Church officials seemed intent on finding a reason to cast doubt on Patrick's ministry. His response to the scandal back home was to write his *Confession*. It is from this declaration (which, incidentally, gives no specific detail about his sin) that we obtain much of our information about Patrick's life. In this work we have such a vigorous tirade against the common practice (even among Christianized Britons) of slave trading that Thomas Cahill refers to Patrick as "the first human being in the history of the world to speak out unequivocally against slavery." There was something profoundly spiritual about Patrick's life as a slave that bound him to that community and served to fuel his intimacy with Christ. His devotional life with God, his service to the despised Irish barbarian and his suffering in a foreign land were mixed up together. In the lives of the suffering he saw the strength of Christ. "But greatest is the suffering of those women who live in slavery. All the time they have to endure terror and threats," wrote Patrick of Christian women who had been abducted into the slave trade. "But the Lord gave His grace to many of His maidens; for, though they are forbidden to do so, they follow Him bravely." Like the emerging friars of today who are seeking to live among and serve twenty-first-century slaves, Patrick gave himself to people about whom the institutional church of the fifth century seemed unconcerned. Seeing the face of Christ in the poor and oppressed, sharing in his sufferings by standing alongside those who are mistreated, and pursing a growing intimacy with Christ by serving at the margins—these are the hallmarks of missionary friars.

BRIGID OF KILDARE

A woman by the name of Brocessa may have been one of God's "maidens" about whom Patrick wrote. She was a slave owned by a wealthy farmer, through whom she got pregnant. Wives whose husbands took concubines felt an understandable sense of competitiveness. But rather than turn on their husbands, they so often turned on the concubine. That was the case with Brocessa. The wife of the chieftain-farmer ordered that the woman be sent away to birth and rear this illegitimate child until the kid could be of some use. So before her daughter, Brigid, was born, Brocessa was sold as a bondswoman to a druid, who was also the child's uncle.

So much legend surrounds the life of St. Brigid of Kildare that it is difficult to divide history from myth. But it is clear that some kind of oddity surrounded the early years of this child of a slave woman. One story recounts an episode from Brigid's infancy. To the surprise of her uncle, Brigid stretched out her hands in the shape of a cross and prophesied quite plainly, "This place will be mine." Whatever the truth about the child, she was eventually returned to her chieftain father at age ten or eleven, and as she grew up, she took to giving away his many possessions to the poor.

Apparently Brigid was a young girl for whom the word *no* had little meaning. When she had a mind to do something (like give out her dad's goods), her father had little power to do anything about it. As a young woman, Brigid insisted on visiting her mother, who remained in slavery to the druid. Suffering from an eye disease, Brocessa was unable to perform her tasks of tending the milk cows and churning butter, so Brigid quickly took upon herself her mother's servile tasks. She would take the portions of milk or butter and divide them into thirteen parts in honor of Jesus and the disciples. One portion was larger than the rest and this she gave to the poor. "Why not save some for yourself?" asked one of the druid's servants. "I find it hard to deny Christ his own food," said Brigid matter-of-factly.

Despite giving so much away to the poor, Brigid's productiveness eventually earned freedom for herself and her mother. In fact the druid owner was

Brigid of Kildare, by Grete Bauder

so taken by her charity that he gave Brigid the cows, which she promptly gave to the poor. Taking her mother to her family of origin in the north of Ireland, Brigid returned to her chieftain father and resumed her mission of distributing her father's wealth to "Christ's brothers and sisters" as she sometimes referred to the poor.

Her father could see that he was a man of quickly diminishing means and decided this kind of disrespect and rebellion was helping neither his financial security nor his social standing as a man who could control his own daughter. Unable to beat Brigid into submission, he threw her into his chariot one day to sell her to the king of Leinster out of sheer frustration. Not wanting to approach the king armed, Brigid's father left his sword in the chariot and went to negotiate a price. During negotiations, a leper came up to Brigid begging. Grabbing the only thing of value she could get her hands on, she gave the leprous beggar her father's sword and sent the man on his way. When her father brought the king out to meet Brigid he soon discovered this plundering act of kindness. "Why do you steal your father's property and give it away?" asked the king. "If I had the power, I would steal all your royal wealth and give it to Christ's brothers and sisters," replied Brigid without the least hint of intimidation.

Brigid, like Clare of Assisi, was a woman of great strength and possessed a tremendous love for the poor. In the poor she found Christ, and in tending to their needs she satisfied her own need for intimacy with her Savior and fulfilled a desire for spiritual devotion. This prayer said before meals is attributed to Brigid:

> I should like a great lake of finest ale
> For the King of kings.
> I should like a table of choicest food
> For the family of heaven.
> Let the ale be made from the fruits of faith,
> And the food be forgiving love.

I should welcome the poor to my feast,
For they are God's children.
I should welcome the sick to my feast,
For they are God's joy.
Let the poor sit with Jesus at the highest place,
And the sick dance with angels.

In time Brigid would become the abbess of a large double monastery of both men and women (the sisters and brothers of the monastery complained like her father that she gave away too many of the monastery's goods). She represents a picture of the Celtic saints who had come from barbarous stock and whose fierceness was reshaped into a deep spirituality that sought to serve Christ in the most extreme ways imaginable.

Many of these young Celtic nuns and monks were extreme ascetics, punishing their bodies in order to submit to radical notions of holiness. Ite, another abbess, kept a stag-beetle under her clothes to gnaw on her flesh, and Kevin of Glendalough, who may have founded the first Irish monastery, spent parts of his life in a cave just four feet wide, three feet high and seven feet deep. These austerities were thought to help beat the desire for worldly things out of a person. Brigid, however, was apparently forbidden by an angel from enduring such extremes; she attempted to mortify her flesh by sub-

> **Without intimacy with Jesus
> we have nothing to give away to others.**

merging in an icy stream only to find the stream dry each evening she purposed to do so. These were men and women bent on discovering a new level of unity with Christ through denial and sacrifice. For Brigid at least, this closeness to Christ was inextricably woven into the fabric of the poor. It was in the poor that Brigid experienced Christ.

Intimacy with Jesus was the passion that gripped Francis and Clare and Patrick and Brigid. It is also the passion of many of the emerging friars of the twenty-first century, men and women driven in their pursuit of the One who walks among the poor. It is him that they seek, for he is so much more than his mission. The philosophy of ministry for Word Made Flesh states that "effective service flows from intimate fellowship with the person of Jesus Christ." Without intimacy with Jesus we have nothing to give away to others. Yet part of experiencing communion with him is connecting our lives to the poor and inevitably suffering. One of the core values for new friars who are laboring under the banner of Servant Partners puts it this way: "As we experience suffering and trials in the course of our mission, we believe that God uses these to refine our faith so that we can rejoice fully when we see him face to face."

The quest for holiness was very near and dear to the Celtic saints. The emerging mission movement to slum communities today shares the devotional intensity of historic orders. But individualistic devotion can be too self-absorbed. To do mission and devotion correctly, the new friars embrace the messiness of community. Indeed community seems to be a hallmark of these new orders that are attracting youth intent on drawing near to Jesus in the disguise of the world's outcasts.

COMMUNAL
Pursuing Relational Wealth

Self-obsession is unavoidable. You might say we're set up to be selfish, exhibiting this trait very early on as babies. And what else would we expect since, as soon as we're born, we can do nothing for ourselves, let alone for other people? Often the first words learned in a typical baby's vocabulary are (1) *Mama,* (2) *Da Da,* (3) *Ball* and (4) *MINE!*

What's amazing to me is that the word *mine* requires such a high level of cognitive functioning—much more so than a simple noun like *cat* or *phone*. *Mine* is an idea, a philosophy, a way of viewing yourself and the world. And as soon as a baby can communicate, this word comes out with passion and deeply intoned meaning.

I feel the idea of "mine" a dozen times a day even if I don't say it. It's *my* house, *my* truck, *my* computer, *my* phone. I even associate the concept with things that are less tangible: it's *my* turf, *my* idea, *my* responsibility, *my* project. Exclusivity is a value to us; we like to attach things to ourselves. There's a level where that's OK. Janine is *my* wife and I am *her* husband; it would be unhealthy to say that she is *our* wife, referring to the broader community of Madison, Wisconsin. It's probably all right to have *my* toothbrush and *my* underarm deodorant—though these things have been shared within our family in dire emergencies. But how far does my notion of personal property extend?

Unrelated Relatives

In the West the idea of a clan with jointly held property is extremely rare— something for "weird" people. But Janine and I tried communal living once, and we liked it quite a bit. An older woman in our church was having trouble keeping up with her house payments, so a few of us moved out of our apartments and in with her. We didn't throw all our income into the same pot, though I know others who do, but we did share our time, space, meals and lives in a way that most people in the West do only with a nuclear family. None of the couples had children at the time, which simplified things a great deal. However, the arrangement ran against the grain of deeply held Western values. We never quite got past the feeling of being a guest in someone else's house. Part of this was due to the fact that the furnishings and décor had been established by our elderly friend, so the aesthetics did not reflect our personality. But even if we had shared together the task of creating a certain feel to the space, I think it still would have been a challenge. We are usually brought up believing that there is at least one room in a house where we have exclusive rights and can do what we want with it. The other difficulty was that five of us had a similar sense of calling to a community ideal while the sixth person was more of a boarder. Families live together without having to ask why. But the expectations in an intentional community such as the one we were in can be quite varied, creating a tension that doesn't exist to the same extent in a traditional family living situation. Still, our memories of those days in community are sweet.

There is something about intertwining our lives with others to the extent that possessions or space or time are held in common that offends Western sensibilities. The new friars, however, don't seem to have quite the same traditional, Western, nuclear family structure notions. Perhaps their community orientation is more biblical. Paul describes the early church in Acts:

> All who believed were together and had all things in common; they would sell their possessions and goods and distribute the proceeds to all, as any had need. Day by day, as they spent much time together in the temple, they broke bread at home and ate their food with glad and generous hearts, praising God and having the goodwill of all the people. And day by day the Lord added to their number those who were being saved. (Acts 2:44-47)

The early Christians so embraced a sense of common identity that it spilled over into their view of property: Why should I be living so well and my sister living so poorly? What if everyone put their "supply" into a big pile and then each took out their "need"? Will it come out evenly? Is there enough between us for everyone to live well if nobody lives opulently? It

> ## Is there enough between us
> ## for everyone to live well if nobody lives opulently?

seems that this is what the first Christians in Jerusalem practiced. Jesus taught them to think of each other in communal terms when he insisted on using nuclear family terms for his followers: "For whoever does the will of my Father in heaven is my brother and sister and mother" (Matthew 12:50). Extended families back then lived together, or at least in proximity. They took care of one another not just with moral support but also material support, sharing resources and spreading the burden of one family member out to the others. So when Jesus encouraged the use of the words *brother* and *sister* among the disciples, they began to transfer the norms for one's natural family to their unrelated "relatives" in Jesus. This intense and intimate fellowship that has its origin in the early church has marked the monasteries and convents throughout history, and it marks the profound sense of community being pursued by the new friars.

SHARING RESOURCES, SHARING SUFFERING

Mike Kingsley, a Wheaton College student at the time of this writing, spent six months living in a slum community in Phnom Penh, Cambodia. He went there as part of Wheaton's Human Needs and Global Resources program and served with Servants to Asia's Urban Poor (Servants), an agency of new friars that plants people in slum communities as agents of transformation. The dwelling Mike lived in with sixteen others was made of concrete, tin, wire mesh and some wood planks. He shared his room with Terra, the oldest of three Cambodian AIDS orphans. Terra is one of the teenage heads of households, a demographic that is exploding on most of the continents outside North America. Part of Mike's mission was to knit himself in, not just into the lives of the other team members serving with his organization, but also into the slum community church with whom Servants works. The church to which Mike belonged functions very much like a family—similar to the community of believers in Jerusalem described in Acts.

Mike Kingsley

Mike blogged one day about an alcoholic in his church family, giving us a picture of their love for each other:

> I followed my host brother up the alley and then down a smaller path, turning the corner to find a part of my neighborhood I didn't know was there. [The dying man we came upon], just a few weeks [prior], was a healthy and active member of our church. He's faced a constant battle with alcohol, but is still a valued member of the community. The last week or so he's been pretty reclusive and has turned back to the alcohol pretty strongly. My pastor found him in this state: He was comatose lying on the ground, in a room with no access to toilet or water. His room was completely filled with rubbish and old clothes (I have no idea where he got all this stuff). He was in a desperate condition and having seizures. He couldn't speak and [was] extremely frail. The church got itself organized and we had about 20

people helping to clean up this house and try and get this man in better condition. The house was in such a mess. All the trash was soaked in alcohol, urine and human excrement. . . . We got half the room cleaned up before dark, on the first day.

The next day, after church, we went back. The man now looked in worse shape and was going through regular seizures (although he looked a bit more responsive). We prayed for him a lot, and did what we could, but he was in a pretty desperate condition (by the amount of medicines and tablets this man had, most of them in unusable condition, I also wouldn't be surprised if he had some other underlying condition). A few of us went home for dinner and then when we came back, we found out that he had died. This was a sad moment. The pastor and his wife were crying (very rare for a society where emotion is not shown like that). We started getting everything in order for the funeral ceremonies. This man had no family nearby and no money to his name (he had a daughter and son, who we got in contact with, but they wouldn't be able to get here until 2 days later, and were just as poor themselves).

I was so proud of my church. For all its other faults, they know the meaning of community and really were this man's family. The following two days we held 3 services a day, where we prayed and sang songs. Some church members took Monday and Tuesday off work (remember these are poor people who need money to get enough to eat). You don't normally take off work even for your good friend's funeral. My host sister said, "He doesn't have any family, we are his only family now." We all took turns sitting by the body (there are lots of traditions and ceremony that go along with the three day funeral preparations) and sitting at the donation table. . . . I learned so much from my church about what community means and what it means to be one family in Christ. They live believing this, and we sing a song that says this every week at church.

Community is central to the identity of Servants to Asia's Urban Poor:

Our workers commit themselves to build community not only with their poor neighbors but also with one another. Wherever possible we work in groups of two or more in a slum community. Teams in each city regularly gather together to nurture their corporate life and equip each other for sustainable ministry. We seek to realize the potential of individuals and groups, and the part they play in the empowerment of their slum community.

Craig Greenfield, international director of this fellowship of urban saints, lived for many years with his wife and children in another slum community in Phnom Penh. He writes, "I learned there was great value in simply listening to people as they gave voice to their suffering." Giving yourself emotionally to a community marked by poverty means you deal constantly with grief and loss. The Greenfields and their colleagues face death regularly. It's part of the communal ideal that marks the new friars.

In 1994 Kristin Jack and his wife, Sue, who served alongside the Greenfields, arrived in Phnom Penh. They prayed that year for the healing of a man in their slum community who was dying. AIDS was still somewhat "un-

Giving yourself emotionally to a community marked by poverty means you deal constantly with grief and loss.

derground" in Cambodia at the time, so they weren't quite certain what had turned a husky Cambodian soldier into a near skeleton. They assumed it was cancer. Before he died, he had a powerful vision in which he met the risen Christ, so he urged his family to turn to Jesus. His wife, Channty, heeded her dying husband's advice and soon endeared herself to the Jacks. She took part in the income-generation business that Servants to Asia's Urban Poor had begun in the community. Her daughter, Sarah, became playmates with the Jack's little boy Kaleb.

In time Channty noticed a growth on her neck that produced a discharge. Kristin and Sue grew concerned, and walked with Channty through the process of obtaining medicine and seeking a cure. A blood test revealed that Channty was HIV positive. The families wept together, prayed and hoped for a miracle. They were bound to each other. Sickness in Channty was akin to sickness in Kristin or Sue or Kaleb. The tragedy only compounded from there. Not long after burying Channty, little Sarah began to show signs of the virus. Sarah died while the Jacks were out of the country. Her remaining relatives did not have the money to bury her in a cemetery, so she was laid to rest in an unmarked grave outside the slum community. Since then, the Jacks have wept many times over people in their community whose lives have been claimed by the runaway virus.

The slum-dwelling friars are learning to live with grief and poverty just as the poor must. Somehow in the middle of it all they are finding that the kindred relationships that bind together their little fellowships help to buoy them through life's tragedies. The believers in slum communities share a hope that their dying friends have gone "where they will be no longer searching for love or justice, but where they will find those things in all their fullness." Sharing poverty, joy, suffering and friendship has added a richness to life for these men and women. They have learned to reach beyond the "mine" mentality with which we are inbred as children, and have discovered an "our" philosophy that embraces hardship, celebration, possessions and living space.

BACK TO KINDERGARTEN

In 2003 Sharmila Blair entered into an apprenticeship with Urban Neighbours of Hope (UNOH) in Melbourne, Australia. The UNOH apprenticeship is meant to test the mettle of the apprentice and to see if he or she is called to a communal life of incarnational service among the poor, much like the novitiate (or novice period) of many historic monastic orders. Living and working alongside drug users, asylum seekers and refugees taught Sharmila the lessons that kindergarten teachers long to teach us but that rarely take root—to share our things and play well with others. Sharmila shared a room with a Sudanese refugee on one occa-

Sharmila Blair, left

sion and, on another occasion, with a single mother and her three kids, all under age seven. "When I walked out of my bedroom," writes Sharmila, "people were there. When I walked into my bedroom, someone was in there sleeping. When I went outside to hang the washing on our communal line, at least three neighbors were doing the same. I desperately tried to find time and space on my own." Sharmila had to work hard to find the balance between the personal and communal, the private and public. But in the process of pursuing a collective lifestyle she found that her relationships became less superficial. She discovered a lavishness to life through communal living with the poor. Now, as she continues to work pioneering a new UNOH neighborhood team, Sharmila has learned how to share, giving away both her heart and her space to her teammates and to the poor among whom they live.

Brian Sze spent the summer of 2002 living in a squatter house with seven other people in Manila, Philippines, as part of the Global Urban Trek. Like Sharmila, he also found himself groaning under the transition from an individualistic life to the kind of closeness inherent in a slum community. "I try to retreat to my bed for some time to myself but there are constantly kids running around, laughing or crying," says Brian. He relates an incident with Nuno, one of the kids in his household.

> *A couple days ago Nuno was looking over my shoulder while I was journaling and reading out loud what I was writing. That made me pretty exasperated, and I asked him if I could just have 5 minutes of time to myself. It took a while for him to understand me but when he did, he just had a look of sadness on his face that made me regret immediately what I had just said. Wanting my personal space here makes me feel like a selfish American. My bed alone takes up more than a third of my family of seven's living space, and for me to think of it as mine is just greedy. But in my heart I cringe when I see the children rolling around in my bed when they're dirty or have rashes or head lice.*

Brian spent the summer wrestling with the questions of community in a stressful environment of poverty and injustice. In the process he found himself being stripped down to his core beliefs about his personal rights, revealing both purity and selfishness in his heart. Randy White, in his book *Encounter God in the City,* speaks about the dead layers of skin that get peeled off as we encounter "disorienting dilemmas" by doing things like moving into the world of urban poverty, intent on tying our lives to our urban neighbors. The emerging order of men and women are finding intense spirituality, deep community and personal transformation in the midst of incarnational mission among the world's outcasts. They seem to me to be forming communities that bleed Jesuit mission when cut.

HEAVEN IN THE JUNGLE

Eastward along the tropic of Capricorn between Asunción, Paraguay, and

São Paulo, Brazil, then southward to Buenos Aires, Argentina, on the Atlantic coast there existed a network of thirty towns surrounded by jungle, dotting the landscape. They were little pictures of heaven populated by Jesuit missionaries and Guarani Indians. The Guarani were once nomadic cannibals constantly on the move or at war with one tribe or another, but they had become followers of Jesus and were living harmoniously with Europeans who were part of a vow-driven organization known as the Society of Jesus, or the Jesuits. In his book *They Built Utopia,* Frederick Reiter asks,

> How had those "Thirty Towns" come into being, the "Jesuit State" in the empty wilderness of Paraguay where a hundred and fifty thousand Guaranies lived peacefully the Christian life, governed by their own officials under the guidance of the fathers, two in each town, in a communal society permeated by the Faith?
>
> Who built the orderly rows of solid houses, the cathedral-like churches, the homes for the widows and orphans? Who shaped the agricultural system and conceived the communal economy? Who created the schools, the workshops of the smiths, carpenters, weavers, painters, and sculptors, the music schools, the choirs and the bands? How had those tightly knit communities been able to survive cruel attacks, carry out vast transmigrations, and to grow and flourish despite all adversities?

Reiter answers these questions by telling the story of the Jesuit mission in Paraguay between 1610 and 1768. It was a mission bent on building communities of faith, inspired by Jesus and the early church. The Jesuits and Guarani owned property together, cared for the needs of the sick and poor among them, and worked communal plantations. A few had roles that exempted them from the fields, like the residents who worked outside the township on the cattle farms in the wide open places known as estancias. But most everyone worked a week in communal fields followed by a week of work in their trade. Communal agriculture allowed widows, orphans and the sick to have a regular supply of food. It was a system that worked very well.

The movie *The Mission,* which is based on the Jesuit mission in Paraguay, includes a scene in which the papal emissary sent to check out the Jesuit communities takes a tour of the mission of San Miguel. He is dumbfounded as he sees the skill with which the Guarani make violins and cellos, the grandeur of their churches, the angelic quality of their voices, the productivity of their plantations. Speaking with the local indigenous priest of San Miguel, he asks where the money from the various economic ventures that year had gone. The priest answers that the money was shared equally by everyone in the town. "Ah, yes," the pope's ambassador replies. "There is a French radical group that teaches that doctrine," referring to Rousseau, Voltaire and others who laid the foundation for the French Revolution. The priest responds matter-of-factly, "Your Eminence, it was a doctrine of the early Christians." The Jesuits had learned early on that the Guarani actually preferred working communally, although each family still had to produce staples from their own plots. Their sharing of resources, skills and land produced thriving communities in the middle of the jungle.

Outside forces, however, threatened their utopia. When they got into the business of producing cash crops to pay taxes or buy supplies, their highly productive communal system began to compete with colonial plantations. So colonial traders in Asunción obtained a ruling that restricted the number of pounds of certain products the missions could sell. The colonial lust for these successful missions also fueled a war to gain control of them by disparaging the Jesuits and feeding the rumor mill. Colonists believed that there were secret gold mines near the townships and that the Jesuits were growing rich from the Guarani.

A prosperous human trafficking industry in São Paulo also made life in the townships difficult. The Paulistas, as they were known, made their living by raiding the jungle tribes and then driving the captured slaves "chained and corded to Sao Paulo, where they were herded into pens and sold like cattle to work on the mines and plantations of sugar, cotton, mandioca and tobacco." The government seemed powerless to stop this trade even if it wanted to—a point that was questionable. The colonists depended on the availability of slaves to mine silver and gold, to run their plantations and to make life so far from Europe more bearable for them. The Guarani suffered immensely at the hands of the slavers. Even the havens they built under the guidance of the Jesuits were not completely safe. In 1630 alone the Paulistas murdered or carried off thirty thousand Guarani from the Jesuit jungle townships. The towns were tempting targets—six thousand potential slaves gathered peacefully together in one place, not scattered about the forest in small hunting bands as other tribes. Consequently, the Jesuits trained the Guarani for armed resistance and obtained weapons for their defense, much to the irritation of the colonists. Preservation of the community was critical. Their sense of identity was so interrelated that an attack on some of them was an attack on all of them.

For 158 years the Jesuits and Guarani flourished in their jungle paradise. However, the turbulent politics of the late 1700s and the insatiable thirst of the colonial economy eventually sucked these missions into their power, expelling the Jesuits and taking control. Shortly thereafter the Guarani re-

> **The interdependence of slum-dwellers puts to shame the kind of shallow relationships that exist in most suburban communities.**

turned to the wilderness or were absorbed into colonial Latin America, and the jungle swallowed the towns as if they had never existed.

But the story of the Jesuit work among the Guarani Indians—their communal legacy—survived and remains a beautiful example of real Christian community: covenantal community where the missionaries and those they serve are bound together.

Slum communities often have this fraternal quality—with or without a Christian presence. The interdependence of slum-dwellers puts to shame the kind of shallow relationships that exist in most suburban communities. For the slum churches being formed by the new friars, this visceral connection with each other runs exceptionally deep. New friars are attempting to speak out against the injustices foisted on their neighbors and "arm" them to resist the forces of intractable poverty that war against them.

CREATING FAMILY

The Jesuits were not the first to come up with the idea of a communal system, nor was Rousseau or Marx. The followers of Jesus lived that way in Jerusalem in the days that followed his departure into heaven. But they were not really trying to develop a new kind of economy or foment a revolution or create a radical social system designed to disempower the nobility. They were simply doing what seemed natural to them: creating a kind of family. Most of the early Christians were entire households that had together turned to Jesus. They embraced other followers of Christ in their city, calling one another "sister" and "brother." They took care of each other materially, emotionally and spiritually as they would any blood relative. The missionary monks and nuns that followed upheld this intensely communal model, sharing nearly all aspects of life together as they traveled and served in foreign places. New friars who have grown up in the West are learning how to give up privatized and individualized expectations for their lives, and in the process they have discovered a sort of wealth that is hard to come by in the affluent neighborhoods: relational wealth.

Part of the radically communal structures they are forming are fueled by the fact that these men and women have left all that is familiar and come to a place that is strange to them. Communal living helps to foster a sense of home and family for those who've left both to adopt a missional lifestyle in pursuit of the kingdom of God.

When someone dies unexpectedly, there is a kind of disbelief that plagues those closest to the deceased. It takes a while to sink in. For days, even weeks, you expect the person to open the door and walk into the room. My big brother Mike died two years ago when he was only forty. A serious fall a couple years before his death had shattered his pelvis. Although doctors were more or less able to put him back together again, he was left with a debilitating pain problem; alcohol was the home remedy that ultimately pushed him toward death. There is a limit to how much whiskey a body can endure day after day. Trouble breathing one afternoon was the start of his organs shutting down. Within fifteen or twenty hours he was dead. I remember laying my hands on his lifeless body in the hospital room and praying quietly that God would raise him back to life. But he just lay there with his eyes closed as if asleep. By the time all the funeral arrangements were complete, the finality of his death had settled in.

Ever since then, I've been seeing random people on the street who look like Mike. It was a little spooky at first, but I'm getting used to it now. I think it's part of the bereavement process—the slow transition from denial to acceptance.

JESUS' LAST WILL AND TESTAMENT

The book of Acts—Luke's record of events following Jesus' death—indicates that Jesus' mom and little brothers were among the early followers: "All these were constantly devoting themselves to prayer, together with certain women, including Mary the mother of Jesus, as well as his brothers" (Acts

1:14). We know that Jesus' mother was near the cross as Jesus was dying, and that he spoke to her briefly as his life ebbed away (John 19:26). She saw him crucified, and very likely she was right there as his cross was lowered and his wilted body was removed. Removing him from the cross seems as if it must have been a bit of an ordeal: holding the dead weight of his body as the beams were carefully lowered to the ground, freeing his hands and feet, pinned to the wood by spikes meant to hold him there. Likely it took a couple of strong men to do the job. By then his body would be cold and his limbs would be starting to stiffen. There would have been no doubt for friends or family who handled his body: Jesus was dead.

Luke tells us a Roman guard poked a hole in Jesus' side with a spear, producing a gush of blood and a spurt of water (probably fluid built up in his lungs), to make sure he wasn't alive. His mom was right there. Do you think she didn't notice the moment when he went limp? She wept just like my mom did, I'm sure of it. His friends and family grieved for him like my siblings and I did for Mike. Those closest to him probably participated in cleaning and preparing the corpse for burial. That was their job. There weren't any mortuaries to rescue loved ones from the gruesome details of handling the dead body of someone close to you.

I can very well imagine how his disciples felt those days he was in the tomb. They may have seen people walking on the streets of Jerusalem that reminded them of their beloved Jesus. So many things trigger memories of a recently deceased relative. Seeing people who look like a dead loved one is startling enough, but to see Jesus walk into the room where grieving friends had gathered must have shocked and frightened them. A twenty-first-century Westerner would assume they were hallucinating. The first-century audience thought he was a ghost: "They were startled and frightened, thinking they saw a ghost. . . . He showed them his hands and his feet. And while they still did not believe it because of joy and amazement, he asked them, 'Do you have anything here to eat?' They gave him a piece of broiled fish, and he took it and ate it in their presence" (Luke 24:37, 40-43 NIV). Jesus didn't ask for food because he was hungry. He wasn't craving some earthly fish after being away from the living for three days. He was trying to convince them that it was really him standing there and not a ghost or an apparition.

The resurrection is the centerpiece of Christian mission. In it, Jesus proved that he was who he said he was: God come to earth to save all humanity. The disciples were joyfully terrified, but they had more than a month to be with Jesus before his ascension. During that forty-day period he delivered his last will and testament. If my brother, Mike, had appeared the day after his funeral, and we were all able to recover from shock and disbelief, you can be sure the things he said to us afterward would be listened to with great attention. So of course what Jesus said to the disciples in those final moments on earth sank deep into their psyche and was written down and passed on. Those last recorded words of Jesus laid a foundation for the mission of all who profess to love and follow him. They are words burned into the soul of missional orders: "Peace be with you. As the Father has sent me, so I send you" (John 20:21).

SEMINARY TRAINING TAUGHT BY THE "THEO" OF "THEOLOGICAL"

For forty days the disciples were enrolled in postresurrection seminary: "After his suffering he presented himself alive to them by many convincing proofs, appearing to them during forty days and speaking about the kingdom of God" (Acts 1:3). The kingdom of God was his teaching obsession before he was crucified. It's partly what got him into trouble in the first place—describing a reality where ordinary people could call Yahweh (whose name could not be spoken or even written) "Daddy." A kingdom like a mustard seed that's nearly microscopic when planted but becomes the biggest plant in the garden. A kingdom like a precious pearl or buried treasure that compels a person to sell everything they own to have it. A kingdom where the poor are rich and the rich are poor, where religious leaders who've spent their lives devoted to the law are called snakes and blind guides and whitewashed tombs but unreligious pagan soldiers are praised for their faith. It was a kingdom that had "here and now" dimensions where God's will is done on earth, just as in heaven. There are other dimensions that are "not of this world" (John 18:36 NIV). Jesus' resurrection mission for his followers is to bring people into this kingdom and to teach them to live it out in this world.

The kingdom of God is a theme of such depth and mystery that even after two thousand years we're still trying to understand it. So far as I am aware, Jesus was the first person on earth to use this phrase. It has become old in our ears, and the word *kingdom* smacks of the monarchies of the Middle Ages for me. But to Jews in the first century the phrase was fresh and strange. A kingdom was not simply a political system—a way of ruling a country. It was a reality that existed as far as a king's reign extended. It grew out of his character. The way a kingdom functioned and the type of place it became changed based on what type of person the king was. The king's personal values became the values for the entire kingdom. When Jesus began saying, "The kingdom of God is like . . ." and then followed with some unexpected metaphor, the people of his day were thinking, *Hmmm. . . . A country where God is the king and the principles and ideals that govern the country come out of who God is.* Hard to imagine. It differs so radically from any country or kingdom we've experienced that we need help wrapping our minds around it. Instead of the powerful occupying high places, it's the meek who rule. Instead of being populated with pious religious leaders like the Pharisees, it's full of people like prostitutes and mafia-like tax collectors who love Jesus and are sorry for their mistakes. What would the environment of a country look like if it were governed by the Creator of the universe? You can bet there would be no slums or endangered species. When Jesus spoke about his Father's kingdom, the poor and lost and broken people wanted it to come right away, here and now, but the rich and powerful weren't so sure it sounded like a place they wanted to be.

The followers of Jesus are residents of this kingdom. Their orders are mostly stated in positive terms. They are taught to pray for this kingdom to come, to seek the kingdom above all else, to tell people it's at hand and to

> **Righteousness and justice are always a double-edged sword: good news to some and bad news to others.**

bring it near to people. But there is also an oppositional role to be played by God's people—though not directed at other human beings. The mission of the church is to confront the counterfeit kingdoms of this world and to usher in a kingdom that is essentially not of this world. God says to Jeremiah, "Today I appoint you to stand up against nations and kingdoms. Some you must uproot and tear down, destroy and overthrow. Others you must build up and plant" (Jeremiah 1:10 NLT). In my mind, this can be applied in a general sense to any who are called to seek first God's kingdom as they encounter evil. In Genesis 1:28 God's first set of commands to the man and the woman included the task of subduing the earth. *Subdue* is a forceful word that is normally used in a military sense. I don't believe this subjugation mission was simply an environmental order, but one that directed men and women to oppose evil and all the works of God's enemy. Paul says that God's people have power to destroy strongholds and "every proud obstacle raised up against the knowledge of God" (2 Corinthians 10:4-5). His kingdom is one of righteousness and justice, and that is always a double-edged sword. It is good news to some and bad news to others. It means bending our world back into the shape God intends, and involves both demolition and construction.

Dismantle the systems that are not aligned with God's character, lift up those at the bottom, put the broken people back together, and teach people to obey God and to believe in his Son: this is the mission of anyone who dares to follow Christ, and it will cost some of those bringing this kingdom their very lives.

SURRENDER ALL

Ash Barker's missionary career flashed before his eyes as he lay in a bed dy-

ing of some illness doctors couldn't identify. He and his wife, Anji, along
with their little daughter Amy had moved into the Klong Toey slum community in Bangkok, Thailand, from their home country of Australia in 2002 in
order to enflesh the gospel among the urban poor there. They knew the cost
of mission to the fringes. They had spent the previous ten years raising up
new friars in Melbourne with Urban Neighbours of Hope, a missionary order they founded (Sharmila Blair, profiled in the previous chapter, belongs
to UNOH). Only six months into their new life in Bangkok Ash grew deathly
ill, and insurance companies were making excuses for why they couldn't pay

Ash, Amy, foster granddaughter Christine, Aiden and Anji Barker

for his hospitalization. Now Anji, who was suffering the early stages of den-
gue fever, lay on the couch next to his bed while Amy did her best to keep
herself entertained with Thai cartoons. The song "I Surrender All" kept ring-
ing in Ash's ears: "All to thee my precious Savior, I surrender all."

I met Ash at the Lausanne Committee for World Evangelization's 2004 forum in Pattaya, Thailand. He was in my issue group on cities. I couldn't help but be drawn to him with his Aussie accent and laid-back manner, his little, round, wire-rim Gandhi glasses, his burly frame and the most genuine smile you could imagine. Some critical years of my childhood—ages nine to eleven—were spent in Australia, so being around Ash brought me back to those years and warmed me. We also shared some of the same disappointments and criticisms of the conference (and of American culture, for that matter). For Ash the setting of the conference stood in stark contrast to his experience of mission. Having spent the last twelve years among the poor and, the most recent years in a Bangkok slum community, it felt jolting for him to participate in an event representing the global church (the majority of which lies in the developing world) held in an opulent five-star convention center planned by a program team almost exclusively from the West. For Ash and Anji and the members of the order they have founded, mission requires immersion into the lives of the least and the lost. Church leaders and missionaries lose touch when their realities differ greatly from the people they serve. Ash writes in his recent book, *Surrender All,* "Few foreign Christian workers in Bangkok today live in the same neighborhoods as those they are serving, never mind learning and seeking transformation from within that community. In fact most live in well-to-do manors and condominiums, complete with maids and gardeners."

> **Church leaders and missionaries lose touch when their realities differ greatly from the people they serve.**

This willingness to surrender all, to give up whatever the Lord asks— whether money or home or health or safety—in pursuit of his kingdom was a mark of the early monastic orders and also marks the new friars today. In 1999 Ash and Anji had spent a three-month sabbatical in Thailand reading, praying and reflecting on what it means to lead a Christian order. They were at a crossroads and needed to get recentered as Urban Neighbours of Hope grew and developed. It was during their sabbatical that Ash threw himself into a study of the historic orders of the church. "Rather than feeling inspired to be part of a new wave of Christian communities," Ash writes, "I felt a wave of tired inadequacy flow over me. 'Who am I to do such a task?' I prayed. 'I know I am lots of things Lord, but I am no Francis or Patrick.'" In his despondence Jesus whispered to him, "You don't have to be someone else. Just light the candles I give you to light." While the missionary impulse runs strong in the new friars and big audacious visions of lighting the world on fire for Christ captivate their imaginations, it is ultimately a spirit of surrender and

Ash and Anji's son Aiden

obedience—a willingness to light one candle at a time—that moves them from person to person, from household to household and from neighborhood to neighborhood, welcoming the kingdom of God as they go.

Ash and Anji both survived their illnesses and now have a little son, Aiden, playing alongside Amy and the children of the Klong Toey slum community who make up their friends and neighbors. There are certainly hazards to slum life for this family and their compatriots, but following Jesus is not safe no matter where he leads you, whether to the halls of power or the alleys of dispossession. And *not following* can actually be dangerous. Disobedience dulls our ears to his voice, and there are soul hazards we don't always take into account by playing it safe. But Jesus' voice will always lead us out of self to the place where he can best use us to further his kingdom.

FOLLOWING CHRIST ONTO THE TRAIN PLATFORMS

It didn't take long after the resurrection for the disciples to discover that following Jesus was the right thing to do even if it came with certain dangers. Some of the disciples found out early on what it meant to relocate themselves from the relative safety of their homes to the mysterious world beyond on their quest to bring God's kingdom to others, just as Ash and Anji did. The pursuit of God's kingdom is a powerfully motivating force, but it is fraught with discomfort, failure, sickness, discouragement and danger. It almost always leads out of the cocoons of familiarity.

Courtney Steever walks among the poor in Kolkata, India, as a missionary with Word Made Flesh. Asking Jesus how he wants her to bring his kingdom is an hour by hour discipline for Courtney. The needs are so great and the resources seem so scant. "Some days it just seems so overwhelming," Courtney confesses. "Often I get tired of the frequent tugs of little hands on my sleeves asking for rupees as I walk down the street. . . . Need is around every corner, under every bridge, down every street—yet it's so easy not to see."

One day Courtney and some other Word Made Flesh missionaries, along with a few Missionaries of Charity, went to the Sealdah Train Station to find those in dire need in order to bring some measure of comfort and relief. The voice of a child called to her, "Auntie, please Auntie." The cries are so incessant there that it's easy to miss them; they're background noise. Courtney did not have enough to give to all who cried out. The little she had was reserved for only the most desperate, so she continued. But so did the voice of the little one. When she finally turned to tell the child that the food was only for those who were sick, she saw instead that the child's pleas were coming from a man of about twenty whose body had degenerated to next to nothing, and who was clothed only with rags. She decided she could spare a hard-boiled egg. It was such a little amount for a person of such great need, but it was what she had to offer. Even a cup of cold water offered in Jesus' name pushes forward his kingdom.

Courtney continued along. Train platforms in Kolkata are very desperate places—the sort of places where those intent on bringing the kingdom of heaven to the least and the lost can be found. A woman begging caught her attention. Courtney noticed her makeshift bandages created from bits of newspaper and scraps of cloth wrapped around wounds on her hand and foot. Jim, a missionary from another organization, stopped with Courtney to re-dress the wounds. The woman smelled of urine and obviously could not walk or stand. She was rotting in her place. The woman held Courtney's hand while her wounds were cleaned. She cried out at first in pain and then in gratitude. Someone had stopped to take notice of her. In that brief moment, the mission of Jesus went forward. His kingdom came to that woman.

Courtney and the others continued their search for the desperate and dying. She came upon a man lying on the ground covered in flies and urine. She and her colleagues helped the man to sit up, feeding him some banana and giving him a little water. They took him in a wheelchair to the home for the dying run by the Sisters of Charity. A few hours later the man died with some semblance of dignity, on a bed and surrounded by people sent to bring the kingdom of God through acts of love. Was Kolkata dramatically changed? No. Did a church emerge as a result of this act of love? Probably not. Did it make any difference at all? It did to that man. The kingdom had come, however small and insignificant it may have seemed to the rest of the world.

> **New friars are drawn to where the kingdom that Jesus described has clearly not yet come.**

It is this missional quest to love and to become as Christ to those who are shut out of the world's systems that drives Courtney and new friar organizations like Word Made Flesh and UNOH to desperate places. They are drawn to locations where the kingdom that Jesus described has clearly not yet come. The great twentieth-century missiologist Lesslie Newbigin describes mission in this way:

Jesus said as he was on his way to the cross, "where I am, there shall my servant be" (John 12:26). The one who has been called and loved by the Lord, the one who wishes to love and serve the Lord, will want to be where he is. And where he is is on that frontier which runs between the kingdom of God and the usurped power of the evil one. . . . At the heart of mission is simply the desire to be with and to give him the service of our lives.

This pursuit of the kingdom has driven so many men and women far from their homes throughout history that the footprints of missionary monks and nuns can be found in corners of the world far away from the origin of the Christian faith.

THE NESTORIAN MISSION MACHINE

When the Jesuits first entered China at the tail end of the 1500s, there were no churches in the imperial capital of Peking. As a matter of fact, there were no known churches anywhere in China at the time. From all outward appearances, Christianity was new to China. However, there were a few distant rumors about a Christian mission to China nearly a thousand years before in the year 635: a missional madman named Alopen, sent by a society of radical monks and nuns from the Eastern church had begun a work that eventually covered China with their footprints and ultimately their blood. Then, in 1623 workmen digging near Xi'an, China, found something that woke a long-forgotten history: a beautiful, black, limestone monument nine feet tall, clearly dated 781 ("the second year of the Chien-chung period" according to the Chinese inscription, which corresponds to the year A.D. 781). Part of its design included a cross rising from a lotus blossom. The monument commemorated more than one hundred years of Christian mission in China, proclaiming that Christianity was "helpful to all creatures and beneficial to all men. So let it have free course throughout the empire." Who were these mysterious ones who had enough clout in China by 781 that they were being celebrated for their contributions to Chinese society and immortalized in a monument? They were Asia's missionary monks and nuns, the Nestorians.

Long before the gospel had come to the Americas, the legacy of Christian mission stretched from Jerusalem through central Asia and the Middle East clear to China. One scholar states, "The church of the East achieved the greatest geographical scope of any Christian church until the middle ages." And the engine for this explosion toward the rising sun was the Nestorian monastic movement. The monastic schools that churned out the Nestorian monks and nuns charged them to go far and wide with the news that Jesus had come to save a lost humanity. John Stewart writes, "Supporting themselves by the labor of their hands or subsisting on roots and fruits or on the grass of the field, they counted no trouble too great, no hardship too severe so long as they might share in the spreading abroad of the message of full salvation for all mankind." Their missionary schools prepared them in fields as diverse as medicine and agriculture, and they were known for their social concerns. Perhaps the best illustration of the geographic breadth of Nestorian mission can be seen in *The Monks of Kublai Khan, Emperor of China,* a book detailing a fascinating journey. The story is from an ancient Syriac manuscript written in the first half of the fourteenth century. It was rediscovered in the late 1800s, and the first complete English translation was made in 1923. In its pages a picture emerges of just how widespread the news of God's kingdom had become in the East, driven by the conviction that Jesus not only saves but also sends.

FROM EAST TO WEST

The Nestorians didn't just go to the East, however. Just as the famous Marco Polo's journey to China and back was coming to an end (1271-1275), another journey was just beginning, only these sojourners were coming from China and heading to the West. Bar Sauma and Marcus were from an Eastern Turkic ethnic group known as the Uighurs (pronounced wee-ger) living in Mongol-ruled China. They were devout Nestorian monks who set out on an adventure to Jerusalem that was at least as marvelous as the Polo family journey. Early on in the trip the great Kublai Khan commissioned them as his emissaries to the kings of the West. Before the final chapter of the chronicle,

Marcus was ordained Catholicos (akin to the pope) of the Eastern church and Bar Sauma would keep company with Emperor Andronicus II in Constantinople (Istanbul, Turkey), then travel on to Paris to visit with King Philip the Fair and to Gascony to see England's King Edward I. In the story of Bar Sauma and Marcus—a tale mostly lost to the West—we see something of the Nestorian spirit of wanderlust, adventure and mission.

Uighur men today

Bar Sauma was born to wealthy parents in Peking, China, around the time of St. Francis's death. His parents were older in years and without a son. They yearned for an heir to inherit their substantial estate so it would not be distributed among strangers and distant relatives. Bar Sauma's birth was credited to their fasting and prayers, which is why they named him Bar Sauma, meaning, "son of the fast." But his parents' delight barely lasted through his teen years. When Bar Sauma turned twenty, he announced his intentions to join a monastery, for "the divine fire was kindled in his heart. . . . He cast away forthwith the shadow of the world, and renounced straightway the desirable things thereof." Like so many of the sons and daughters of aristocracy of whom I have already spoken—Francis, Clare, Patrick, Brigid and some of the Jesuits of rich European stock—Bar Sauma wanted more from life than the pleasures that money could buy. He wanted spiritual depth—the kind that comes by making friarlike vows and by the denial of earthly wealth, not through indulgence. Becoming a Nestorian monk seemed the best route available to a young Christian man living in medieval Peking.

His parents poured on the guilt: "Ponder well who will be made the master of the produce of our toil. How can it possibly be pleasing to thee for our seed and name to be blotted out?" It worked. Bar Sauma stayed home and attempted to bury his dreams of a life devoted to Christ as a monk. But guilt is rarely an effective tool in permanently changing behavior. Three years later his parents saw that they could no longer bottle his passion, and they released him. Bar Sauma sold everything he had, gave the money to the poor and donned the garb of a monk, shaving his head in the monastic tonsure reminiscent of the Nazirite vow (Numbers 6).

After a few years of life in a monastery, he decided he was ready for the solitary life. After a day's journey from Peking he found himself at a cave near a spring of water—just the place for a thirteenth-century spiritual recluse. In short order, news of his highly disciplined and saintly character began to attract others. Marcus, probably a teenager at the time, was among those who sought out Bar Sauma to guide him in his own spiritual direction and to assist him in his quest to be a monk. But Bar Sauma was reluctant, claiming, "Even the old and experienced monks endure the hardness thereof with the greatest difficulty; shall I permit youths and children to journey on it?" But apparently Bar Sauma wasn't the only persuasively stubborn young person who ever embarked on a mission to follow Jesus with abandon. So Marcus prevailed upon him.

Marcus and Bar Sauma bound themselves together with a pledge to remain companions, come what may, in a perilous journey to Jerusalem. The story of their trek is not about planting new outposts of the kingdom where there were none. That was the quest of their predecessors in the centuries leading up to their own. The story of Marcus and Bar Sauma is really a testament to the missionary enterprise of their forefathers and foremothers. Think about it: a pair of Chinese Uighur Christians in the thirteenth century traveled west from Peking and were welcomed by brothers and sisters in the faith at nearly every point in their journey all the way to Baghdad, the "Vatican" of the Eastern church. The account of the travels of these two products of Nestorian mission gives us an appreciation of the extent and success of Nestorian monks. When Marcus was made supreme patriarch of the Eastern church at age thirty-five, the geographic scope of his rule was far larger than the pope in Rome at that time. He was in charge of a church that stretched from Syria to China and from northern Mongolia to the southern tip of India. The young men and women who made up the Nestorian mission movement were not at peace unless they were on the move, planting mission-centered monasteries.

WHEN THE MISSIONARY BECOMES A MISSION FIELD

What is it that transforms a vibrant mission sending community into a community that has somehow forgotten the name of Jesus and needs to rediscover him all over again? I'd say, "Ask me in another one hundred years when that process has been completed in the West." It's easy to talk about the rise of a particular civilization or the growth of the church among a certain people. The truth is, nobody really knows what happened in central Asia that erased much of the work of the Nestorian church. Of course everybody has their opinions. On the one hand the Nestorians could be too accommodating, so that the teachings of Jesus and the distinctiveness of following the risen Christ blended unhelpfully into the fabric of Buddhism and Confucianism and became indistinguishable. On the other hand the Persianness of Nestorian Christianity never really came to be owned by the other ethnic groups of the region. There was never a truly Mongol or Uighur expression of Christianity. It was always dressed in Persian clothes. Whatever the cause, by the time the Jesuits got to China much of the Christian faith had disappeared. The demise of the Nestorian missionary communities serves as a warning to those new orders following in their footsteps.

> **Intimacy with Christ must come first, but some form of mission will soon follow.**

For all my emphasis in chapter six on the need to pursue Christ over his mission, the truth is that one does not have real intimacy with Christ for very long without wanting others to join in. Intimacy with Christ must come first, but some form of mission will soon follow. The coming friars, like Ash and Anji Barker and Courtney Steever, who are living in the slum communities of the world, are possessed of a Nestorian-like quest to saturate the ground with the kingdom of God. They will not be satisfied to see it come locally or partially. They want it wholly and they want it globally. And until the earth is filled with the knowledge of the glory of the Lord they will give the dark places of our world no rest—even at the expense of their own marginalization by the mainstream.

MARGINAL

Pursuit at the Edges

One of the most feared phrases an introverted, extremely shy, junior high school boy can hear in a room full of peers is "OK everybody, divide into teams." For some unfathomable reason, when I was in sixth grade I decided to join a bowling league. I was a quiet, somewhat insecure kid, and my family had just returned to Iowa after living in Australia for two years. When the announcement came over the speakers to form teams I cringed. I only knew one person in the group, and he quickly distanced himself from me and got together with his buddies. After the chaos of about seventy or eighty kids running around to find their friends had settled down, all of us "rejects" stood along the walls looking at one another. There was a guy who was slow and had been held back a grade or two, another kid who was unusually tall and awkward, and one boy who had mild cerebral palsy. Those of us without a team became a team unto ourselves. For the life of me, I cannot remember the name we chose for our little crew of outcasts. All I can remember is the name with which we were branded by all the other teams. They called us "The Retards." We were unpopular. We were the subject of cruel jokes. We were ignored by the cool kids. We were presumed to be horrible bowlers. And we claimed third place in the tournament that year!

All social structures have margins—places just on the outside of acceptability. At any given time in any given culture there are people on the outside and people on the inside. My bowling team was made up completely of those on the social fringe. All of us have been on the outside at one time or another. We know the feeling of being considered "out" by the "in" group. Society's edges are lonely; we often work hard to get to the inner circle and

stay there, because social ostracism is no fun. The preaching orders of old
and new friars, however, don't care so much. Like their Old Testament Nazirite forerunners, they thrive on being set apart and sometimes set aside.
You might say they gravitate to the edges like items being spun around in a
centrifuge. There is a natural pull to the very outer boundary.

Josh Maxwell

Josh Maxwell spent a summer working with InnerCHANGE on the
streets of San Francisco. He and his team worked in the Haight-Ashbury
neighborhood and even spent time living out on the streets so as to step
into the reality of the lives of those whom they served. They called their
group "The Outer Circle." Since then, Josh has continued to serve marginalized people. He now works with Servant Partners, living and ministering
in a Muslim country among a group of formerly nomadic people who have
been forced by drought to form a squatter settlement in a poor urban area.
They are scraping together a living as best they can as outcasts. Josh says
of the people he lives and works among, "No matter how poor my neighbors may be I can not define them by their poverty and their needs, be-

cause God defines them first as his children."

Most of the historic mission orders found themselves bound to people at the margins: the desperately poor, the "uncivilized," plague victims, lepers, slaves, outcasts—people whom nobody else really wanted to be around. The "in" group marked boundaries and built walls, which the monks and nuns of old spent a good deal of their time climbing over. As a result, these orders sometimes found themselves marginalized by the wider church.

The new friars are also placing themselves alongside people on the margins. For the most part they too are peripheral to mainstream church life. The social activism and prophetic voice of the new friars are often kept outside the center of wider church. Their love for people who have fallen to the outer ring of society comes from a long-standing and historic tradition of disciples who loved surfing the edges. Today's Western church relegates them to the periphery. We've forgotten that some of Christianity's best years have been spent outside the bounds of popularity.

> **Some of Christianity's best years have been spent outside the bounds of popularity.**

BUG-EATING CAVEMAN

Sometime around the year 0, a baby boy was born in an obscure Jewish community. His birth occurred under miraculous conditions. The angel Gabriel visited his father and told him his son would bring many of the people of Israel back to the Lord. And of course, his prophecy came true. This son had an amazing ministry and said many profound things. A group of disciples followed him as he went around proclaiming, "Repent, for the kingdom of heaven has come near" (Matthew 3:2). When he was in his thirties people began responding to his message in droves, but at the height of his ministry he was executed by a political leader. Jesus of Nazareth, right? Nope; meet John the Baptist.

John was a bug-eating caveman and a Nazirite from birth. You don't get more fringe than that. Prophets and Nazirites were like that—out of the bounds of what you'd call normal. John fit the mold of the Jewish cave monks of the first century who dunked people in water to symbolize spiritual cleansing. But he was different than the prophet-wannabes of the day who tried to raise a revolt against Roman political tyranny. Those so-called prophets never amounted to much. But Jesus Christ said of John, "Truly I tell you, among those born of women no one has arisen greater than John the Baptist" (Matthew 11:11).

John the Baptist had such a significant impact on people that when Paul arrived in Ephesus a good twenty years after John had been beheaded, he came upon a group of people who followed John's teachings and knew only of John's baptism, not Jesus' (Acts 19:1-7). As a matter of fact, there is a group of people today known as the Mandaeans, living predominantly in Iran and Iraq, who follow the teachings of John the Baptist while at the same time rejecting orthodox Christianity.

John the Baptist was an intriguing figure. He looked in his day a little like some of the kingdom-bringers who have followed look to those in the center—like a freak. John wore clothing made from the carcass of a camel and lived on free-range grasshoppers and organically produced honey. He didn't need money for his food, clothing and shelter because he was something of a caveman. If his message hadn't been so captivating he might have been accused of being mentally ill. Actually, some did say he was possessed by a demon (Luke 7:33). People on the fringe are a curiosity, especially if they are deeply religious and inspiringly articulate. Some of the new friars living among the poor today are like that. People are uncomfortable around them at times because of their radical lifestyle, but their message of Jesus' revolutionary love for the outer circle also draws people to them.

Crowds came to hear what John had to say and then would let him submerge them in water to symbolize their commitment to be morally clean. He certainly wasn't winsome with his words: "John said to the crowds that came out to be baptized by him, 'You brood of vipers! Who warned you to flee from the wrath to come? Bear fruits worthy of repentance'" (Luke 3:7-8). But he touched something in people. A revival hurricane swirled about him. To those coming to see a freak show or to be baptized for appearance's sake, his words were harsh. But others were sincerely moved, particularly those who also existed on the fringe of orthodox Jewish society, like tax collectors and Roman soldiers (soldiers were as "outside" in the minds of orthodox Jews as American soldiers in Iraq are to devout Muslims): "Even tax collectors came to be baptized, and they asked him, 'Teacher, what should we do?' He said to them, 'Collect no more than the amount prescribed for you.' Soldiers also asked him, 'And we, what should we do?' He said to them, 'Do not extort money from anyone by threats or false accusation, and be satisfied with your wages'" (Luke 3:12-14).

We don't have tax collectors today—at least not like the ones in first-century Palestine. But just imagine if your country had been taken over by a powerful neighboring empire bent on controlling any entity, commercial or political, that it thought it might be able to use for its own self-indulgent interests. (If you're American you'll just have to pretend that your country is not that empire.) Defeated and demoralized, you are maddened that one of your own kinsman has sold out and begun collecting *your* taxes for this money-sucking empire. He can tell you whatever tax rate he wants, and take all the money over and above your real rate for himself—and nobody will check his math or hold him accountable. Of course you'd despise him. In the eyes of the patriotic Jew, tax collectors were scum. Roman soldiers were worse. They were the enemy. Because they were so poorly paid, they used the point of their spear to make up any reason they could to "fine" others. So to the devout Israelite, tax collectors were bottom-feeding traitors and soldiers were the stupid lunks who kept a corrupt system in place by bully power.

Outcasts are often drawn to one another. These tax collectors and soldiers were some of the people on the outer circle of Jewish society drawn to John, and John was drawn to them (at least to those whose hearts were repentant). They formed a fellowship on the fringe that apparently offended certain powerful people. Jesus said to the mainstream religious leaders, "Truly I tell you, the tax collectors and the prostitutes are going into the kingdom of God ahead of you. For John came to you in the way of righteousness and you did not believe him, but the tax collectors and the prostitutes believed him; and even after you saw it, you did not change your minds and believe him" (Matthew 21:31-32). Prostitutes were another one of those societal rejects who constantly raised eyebrows for both Jesus and John, particularly among the "in" groups—and those with wealth and power are almost always on the inside.

Herod was wealthy and powerful—and he was also corrupt; his wife, Herodias, was conniving. Riches and power can bring immorality, and people whose lives or livelihoods can be destroyed by those in power will often keep their mouths shut. People on the margins, however, have a freedom that socially respectable people don't have. When you're outside of the "in" group, you don't have to worry about your reputation. John therefore felt a freedom, or maybe even a holy compulsion, to blast Herod for marrying his own sister-in-law, and for all the ways he abused the power God had given him (Luke 3:19). Those of us who live in places where freedom of speech is practiced have perhaps grown accustomed to being able to verbally bash a political leader or two. But John lived almost eighteen hundred years before any of the revolutions that cemented democracy. Back then, people simply didn't say anything bad about a king—not in public anyway.

Despite John's criticisms and the fact that he was on the edge of society, Herod did seem to have some kind of respect for him. After Herod had John imprisoned he would bring him out to play for a bit, like a toy, inviting John to preach to him (Mark 6:20). Herodias, however, had no such interest in listening to John. She bided her time for a moment of weakness in her husband so that she could somehow have John killed. On Herod's birthday their daughter (also named Herodias) danced. Details are sparse, but I don't imagine a little girl doing her tap routine for the guests. I imagine more of a popping-out-of-the-cake kind of dance at a bachelor party. By the end of the performance Herod was falling over himself to give her some kind of lavish gift in front of everyone ("up to half his kingdom" was a phrase that probably meant "ask for any outlandish present within my power to give and it's yours"). Such an incredible offer required a consultation with her mother.

The girl must have already had everything she wanted, because instead of asking for a new horse or new clothes, she asked for John's head to be presented on a platter right then and there. In an honor/shame society, the powerful don't promise to give someone anything they want in front of a group of important guests (all the "in" people) and then back down. John's gruesome death was a form of entertainment for a party. More than that, it was the result of the corrupt and powerful taking offense at the truth-talking fringe. And if John was fringe, then Jesus must have been too, because Jesus reminded Herod of John. He even thought Jesus was John back from the dead! Those called to minister at the edges are bound to face misunderstanding and rejection by the "popular," just as did Jesus and John.

> **Those called to minister at the edges are bound to face misunderstanding and rejection by the "popular."**

CHURCH OF THE TRANSVESTITES

The prostitutes and outcasts in Palestine that brought such scandal to Jesus and John are hanging around the new friars as well. Anyone drawn to the slum communities of Phnom Penh can hardly avoid the pervasive sex industry. But caring for and working with prostitutes is the kind of association that can ostracize you.

All five of the organizations of slum-dwelling new friars mentioned in this book are working with prostitutes. Southeast Asia seems especially rife with sex trafficking. Local observers say that the prostitution business really began to take off during the Vietnam War era when a large influx of U.S. troops with money to burn entered the cash-poor communities of Cambodia, Vietnam and Thailand looking for recreation. Servants to Asia's Urban Poor (Servants) runs an AIDS education program in Phnom Penh. Last year three hundred men and five hundred women came through their training. Recently a teenage boy visited their program. He was a transvestite who knew next to nothing about the risks his lifestyle had exposed him to. Kristin Jack, the Asia coordinator for Servants who works with this program, writes, "Shyly, he asked whether Servants would allow his friends to come and learn what he was learning. Not really knowing what we were in for we agreed and thought nothing more of it. The next week a large group of flamboyantly dressed young men and boys arrived at our tiny office and applied themselves to learning how to protect themselves over the next few weeks."

The flow of prostitutes and transvestites in and out of churches and ministries must be somewhat damning as looked upon by those in the wider church, especially since Servants hands out condoms. People wonder, *doesn't this aid and abet prostitutes in their trade?* It's easy to cast stones from the comfort of one's limited frame of reference. But in the thick of the battle, you do what makes the most sense from the vantage point of the trenches. I once visited Rahab Ministry, an outreach to prostitutes in Bangkok. They have opened up a beauty shop in the Patpong district, one of the most notorious red-light districts in the city. The volunteers with Rahab do up the prostitutes before they go out. At first glance this seems counterproductive for an organization determined to deliver prostitutes from a life of selling their bodies to strangers. However, in the process of making up prostitutes, Rahab workers (some of them former prostitutes themselves), have been able to build relationships of trust among the sex workers of Patpong. They have introduced many of their prostitute friends to Jesus and have called them to a better way of life, not from a position of superiority, but from a position of friendship.

To be sure, Servants to Asia's Urban Poor views sex trafficking as a blight on society and urge prostitutes to leave their profession. But it's not really that simple. The sex industry in the developing world is very often a form of modern-day slavery. Estimates show that more than half the prostitutes in Cambodia were illegally sold into prostitution, sometimes by a family member. Many of the prostitutes are teenagers, and there are even young children caught in the business. Helping commercial sex workers or children leave the brothel is not easy. Pimps and brothel owners do not look kindly on those who run away. There's a lot of pressure to stay in the brothel. Even those abducted against their will end up, in time, preferring to stay among their friends rather than face the hazards of living on their own outside. Poverty is perhaps the cruelest taskmaster, keeping prostitutes active in plying their trade because of the insurance it provides their families. If they remain in the brothel, they know their children or their parents will have a life of only modest deprivation instead of utter destitution.

> **Sometimes funding becomes unavailable if your ministry's programs might be viewed as useful to prostitutes.**

Servants' team members must first win prostitutes and transvestites to an understanding of Jesus' love for them by living out his love in tangible ways. Their heart's desire is that they escape a life of servicing customers with their bodies. These slum saints work to train prostitutes in other trades. But things like love and trust and friendship take time, so while their prostitute friends are still active in the trade and deciding what to make of their Christian confidants, a condom may simply be saving their life or the life of the HIV-positive child they will bear. Servants' workers in Phnom Penh are frankly tired of burying so many of the people in the slum communities that they have grown to love. But their close relationships with prostitutes and transvestites have set them up for disdain and exclusion by many people. Sometimes funding becomes unavailable if your ministry's programs might be viewed as useful to prostitutes in their work. In Cambodia, for example, "NGOs discontinued plans to provide English language training classes for people working in the commercial sex sector for fear such programs would be interpreted as 'promoting prostitution,'" making them ineligible for funding.

In the church, we sometimes do the same thing, distancing ourselves from those who befriend the people we feel deserve to be on the margins. The attitude seems to be, "let them first learn to live righteously, and then they can come to church." But that was not the posture of Jesus. The emerging missionary communities in the slums of the twenty-first century press ahead into these abandoned places, often in spite of both rejection by the wider church and physical danger.

THE INCREMENTAL COST OF SERVICING THE OUTER CIRCLE

Ministry to the margins has a kind of glamour that those ministering in the mainstream either resent or long for. Gangs, prostitutes, prison, slums—it all sounds so exciting, like it would make great fodder for storytelling and family news letters. But the glam factor is short-lived when the daily grind of life among the poor sinks in. InnerCHANGE founder John Hayes experienced that feeling when he was dropped off by a vanload of volunteers in 1983 after he made the decision to live in a high-poverty, high-crime L.A. neighborhood: "As John watched the van pull away, he experienced a moment of frustrating clarity and conviction. He saw that good-hearted Christians doing 'commuter' ministry were conveying but little impact, that driving down and driving into people's lives were two very different propositions." Less than a year later he left the organization he was with because he could no longer pursue a ministry style that was top-down and resource-driven. That is why he started InnerCHANGE, choosing instead an incarnational ministry devoted to the margins.

Not long after, John Hayes was joined by two more InnerCHANGE missionaries willing to "drive into" people's lives: John and Birgit Shorack. They worked for fifteen years in a location where gunshots were routinely heard. Raising their family in inner-city L.A., they learned how to face those kinds of risks with a certain amount of composure. Then in 2001 John and Birgit moved with their three kids—Johanna, Marna and Mark—into a barrio (slum community) in Caracas, Venezuela. They had formed a relationship with a Venezuelan missionary order that served among the poor, Operación

Timoteo. John was eager to help train and release Venezuelan slum-dwelling friars into ministry around the world. A team soon formed and took up residence in a Caracas barrio.

John had a saying that kept the reality of violence in perspective: "Anything can happen at any time, though most things won't happen most of the time." But the daily violence of living in the margins wears down perspective. Once the whole family was caught up in a street riot; a man with a gun played the role of angel and helped the family escape safely. A nearby barrio where the team is developing ministry is notorious as one of the most violent neighborhoods in all of Caracas. The toll of violence on that community is in their face regularly as they walk in and out of the area. John and a team member were held up at gunpoint just fifty meters from his home. Another time John was mugged with his nine-year-old middle child, Marna, present. Twice John has been robbed while riding on a bus. A bus driver was murdered on a bus line the children take to and from school. John writes:

> *Something happened to me as a result of these experiences, though I didn't realize it until later. I became emotionally traumatized. I found myself consumed with the notion of dying. My mind would wander to my childhood and the loss of my father when I was six years old. From there my mind would turn to my own children; "Lord," I would pray with tears welling up from deep inside, "I don't want to die yet! I don't want to leave them without their Dad." . . . For the first time in my life, in Caracas, I felt confused and insecure. I continued my community work in the poor hillside barrios. While taking greater precautions, I continued walking the hillside, visiting homes and riding public transportation.*

John, Birgit and their team know that life for the other residents in their barrio is no different. Many are captive to fear and so the team must find their way through fear to the other side. They have bound their destinies to the destinies of the poor in Caracas. With the conviction that Jesus is real and alive today and that he cares passionately about the poor and oppressed, they forge ahead on society's outer circle. Bit by niggling bit, their sense of safety and their patience is assaulted. But as they move forward, they beat down a path along which others may follow.

The Shorack family is on the fringe, where few individuals, let alone families, choose to go voluntarily. Servants' team members who are working among the prostitutes and transvestites in the slum communities of Phnom Penh also face raised eyebrows when describing their lives to "normal" people. The historic orders we've looked at in this book have often born the scorn of society at large, and even of the church. The Celtic monks were held at arm's length by the Roman church, the Nestorians were called heretics, the early Franciscans were considered too harsh in their lifestyle and the Jesuit order was dissolved by the pope in 1773 for more than forty years. But on the outer edge of the outsiders were the Moravians.

THE CITY OF BROTHERLY HATRED

Ten-year-old Anna Nitschmann knew what it meant to be an outcast. Kids don't generally choose the religion of their family, and Anna was born into a *Unitas Fratrum* family in the Czech Republic (back when it was called Moravia). *Unitas Fratrum* meant the "Unity of the Brothers," and it was a radical Christian sect with a serious history of martyrdom. Anna's family was part of this underground Protestant sect in Catholic Moravia in the 1700s, which meant they were not only marginalized, they were also actively oppressed. Our friends the Jesuits, sadly, were leading the charge in Europe, tracking down and torturing heretics like Anna's dad, who did time in prison for wanting to follow the teaching of Scripture even when it conflicted with the teachings of the Catholic Church. John Foxe's *Book of Martyrs* gives gruesome descriptions of the fate of Unitas Fratrum founder John Hus and some of his followers. Anna did not ask to be a so-

cial reject, nor did she ask to be a refugee. But in 1725, while her father
and brother were in jail, the rest of
the Nitschmann family decided
to get out from under the
thumb of the Catholic Haps-
burgs and find asylum in some
Protestant land.

Word had been floating around
about a safe haven for religious refugees in Lutheran Germany (though
some Lutherans did their fair share
of persecuting Anabaptists like the

Anna Nitschmann, by Grete Bauder

Mennonites), so the Nitschmanns decided to join a growing community of
outcasts on the grounds of a generous count, Nicolas von Zinzendorf. A
few years prior to their coming, Count Nicolas decided that his Christian
faith was all talk and no action. So when a Unitas Fratrum refugee named
Christian David asked if he could squat on Zinzendorf's estate, the twenty-
two-year-old count decided this was his chance to put his faith into practice. Christian David moved onto the property at Zinzendorf's encouragement and soon invited some of his brothers and sisters to camp out with
him. By the time Anna's family arrived in 1725 there were ninety people
in a squatter settlement on Zinzendorf's land. They turned the swampy
grounds a mile outside of Berthelsdorf (the town that had grown up
around Zinzendorf's castle) into a little colony. The refugees were mostly
of working-class stock and had the basic skills to put together a makeshift
village, which they dubbed "The Lord's Watch," or *Herrnhut*. A year and a
half after the Nitschmanns arrived, the squatter settlement had grown
from ninety to over three hundred. Since these were religious fanatics who
had paid dearly to speak out against Catholic Christianity, they now exercised their freedom to disagree with one another: "As the settlers learned
to know each other better they learned to love each other less. As poverty

crept in at the door love flew out of the window." The Lutheran church in Berthelsdorf that the squatters attended began to resent this factious group of refugees disturbing their peace.

By age twelve, Anna had had enough of the kind of religious zeal that had brought her family so much trouble and, most likely, of the division among the asylum seekers. When someone from the community attempted to convert Anna, she would tell them to go convert themselves. Then in the summer of 1727 the Holy Spirit swooped down upon them all.

Zinzendorf had become concerned that the bickering was going to destroy the refugees along with his Berthelsdorf community. The Unitas Fratrum were anything but "Unitas," so Zinzendorf preached a three-hour sermon on unity that struck a chord with the little flock. The pastor at the Berthelsdorf Lutheran church invited the Herrnhut community for a communion service on August 13, 1727, to restore fellowship between the various warring parties. Confessions began and weeping erupted. To everyone the nearness of God's presence was palpable. People were on their faces, prostrate in utter repentance. It was a festival of penitent wailing where no one was left unscathed—a good old-fashioned revival meeting that has been hailed as the Moravian Pentecost. Several days later a similar revival swept through the children's service. After that, Anna was different. She now embraced the faith with all her energy.

That summer the community decided that for any given day, twenty-four men and twenty-four women would each take an hour to pray. They did this twenty-four hours a day, seven days a week, for one hundred years. From that summer of 1727 forward their identity as a fellowship—distinct from Roman Catholics, and even distinct from Lutherans—had been forged. They really were the Unitas Fratrum once more, though because so many were from Moravia they simply became known as the Moravian church. Their prayer meeting would fuel one of the greatest mission movements to the margins of the planet the church has ever known. "In its singleness of aim," Kenneth Scott Latourette says of the Moravian church, "it resembled some of the monastic orders of the earlier centuries." Moravians were hungry people. They knew hardship and marginalization, and it gave them a passion for prayer, for the kingdom and for the outer edges.

CHILDLESS MOTHER

The young Moravian men and women as well as the widows and widowers each lived in separate households and drew lots to identify a leader who would be responsible to direct their affairs and represent them to the larger community. When the time came to determine the eldress over the young women of Herrnhut, the lot fell to fourteen-year-old Anna. The count thought it was highly irregular for a child to occupy such a key position of leadership, so he urged Anna to turn down the role. But it seemed wrong to Anna to say no to God, who had directed the outcome of the lot. So at an age when most kids today are just leaving middle school, Anna became a leader in the Moravian community. Since the Moravians were far more egalitarian than most congregations of the day, this meant that little Anna not only spoke into the lives of the single women over whom she had charge, but also spoke into the affairs of the entire community alongside her counterpart in the single men's household as well as the leaders of the other households. In 1746 Anna was named mother of the entire Moravian church, becoming known simply as "mama," although she never bore children to the day of her death.

Anna began her reign by leading the single sisters into a covenant "that henceforward they would not make matrimony the highest aim in life, but would rather, like Mary of Bethany, sit at the feet of Christ and learn of Him." Though this was not a vow of celibacy, Anna had opportunity to put this oath into practice. As time moved on, Anna turned down two marriage proposals and watched many of the single sisters in her household marry boys from the household of single brothers. Her aim was to be a devoted student of Jesus first and foremost, and in many ways her singleness allowed a mobility that married sisters did not enjoy. Anna's role became apostolic. She traveled extensively since the Moravians burdened themselves with the fate of slaves and indigenous people in the Americas, the West Indies, South Africa and other locations. Anna went with Zinzendorf and others as they helped establish communities like Herrnhut around the world. At twenty-five she sailed to America where she ministered from community to community in Pennsylvania. "So as not to be a burden to the hard-working people among whom she missionated, she assisted them in the labors of the house, and of the farm; for Anna Nitschmann was the daughter of a peasant, and had often watched her father's sheep in the pastures of Kunewalde."

She did marry, quite late in life by eighteenth-century standards or even by today's. She was forty-one when she wed Zinzendorf of all people, a year after his wife had died. The idea of a count marrying the daughter of a peasant was so scandalous that they kept their marriage a secret from the German nobility for a year. Three years after their marriage the count died, and Anna followed ten days later. Except for her lengthy periods of travel, Anna served as head eldress of Herrnhut from age fourteen until her death in 1760 more than thirty years later.

Though she was bright and skilled as a leader, Anna was unknown to anyone but the Moravians. She was an enigma in the Christian world at the time. In the 1700s, women simply did not have governance roles within the church. In fact, shortly after Zinzendorf's and Anna's deaths, under pressure from within and without, the Moravians backpedaled on women in leadership and fell in line with mainstream Christianity, prohibiting women from having the kind of governance role that Anna exercised over the whole Moravian church.

Born into a peasant family, living within a persecuted, "fringe" religious community, serving as an apostle and traveling throughout the world at a time when very few people crossed countries let alone oceans, giving leadership to the global Moravian community from age fourteen onward when women were relegated to child-rearing roles—Anna Nitschmann lived her life on the outer rim of "normal" eighteenth-century society. But life at the margins *was* normal to Moravians.

SLAVES TO GOD'S MISSION ON THE MARGINS

In a book attempting to draw a line between missional monastic movements of the past and today's emerging orderlike mission structures, you might think it strange to include a chapter on a Protestant sect. Clearly the Moravians would not define themselves as an order in the sense that the Franciscans do. Still, the connection is not as odd as it may seem. The great evangelical abolitionist William Wilberforce compared the Moravian missionary effort in the West Indies to the Jesuit missions in Paraguay. In fact, like the Jesuits, the Moravians lived essentially in missionary settlements, intent on raising up and sending out from their communities numbers who would traverse the world in the attempt to plant colonies on the edges of the "civilized" world. This is what formed the foundation for their Christian community. The least and the lost were the holy obsession of the Moravians, who sent wave after wave of missionary squads to some of the harshest environments on the planet: to the native people in Arctic lands, to the Hottentots of South Africa, to Tibetans of the Himalayas, to slaves in the West Indies and to dozens of other locations. They paid a price for their compulsion. If they survived the journey to the margins many died on the field, especially in the early years of a mission settlement.

The West Indies was a harsh place to live in the 1700s, and few journeyed there unless by slave ship. Among black slaves the death rate was higher than the birthrate, generating a massive slave market as many needed to be imported to fill in the ranks of the dead. In June of 1734, burdened by the

> **The least and the lost
> were the holy obsession of the Moravians.**

plight of slaves, four women and fourteen men landed on St. Thomas on their way to St. Croix in the West Indies. They were reinforcements for two Moravian missionaries who had arrived a year and a half prior. By January, eight of the eighteen were dead, giving new meaning to the term *short-term* mission. In February another eleven people set out as reinforcements from

Herrnhut, five of whom died within two months of their arrival (including the doctor sent to help them survive). Over the next two years most of those who managed to stay alive returned to Europe, three of whom were shipwrecked on the way back. Those who remained eventually succeeded in establishing a thriving Moravian mission.

The Moravians were indefatigable. They kept sending out missionaries to face certain hardship because they were so thoroughly concerned about people to whom few others gave any heed. Their missionary burden for slaves started when Count Nicolas met Anthony, a Christian slave, who described to Zinzendorf the state of his kin in the Danish West Indies. Nicolas was moved and inspired, and thought that surely some from Herrnhut could establish a community there and bring news of the Savior to the slaves. Nicolas brought Anthony to Herrnhut to address the fellowship, and in short order a pair of Moravian brothers had decided to relocate to the West Indies.

Anthony was convinced that it would be extremely difficult to bring any sort of Christian message unless the missionaries were to become slaves themselves. Slaves on sugar plantations worked long hard days and had very little time for sitting around and shooting the breeze with some German-speaking whites from across the ocean. However, out in the fields and in the shacks at night there might be opportunity to bring word of the Savior. Despite the Moravian brothers' willingness to enslave themselves to a plantation owner, Danish law prohibited them to do so. Still, within eighteen months of Anthony's appeal the first two Moravians had arrived and found lodging on a plantation in St. Thomas.

To recount the history of Moravian work among the slave communities in the West Indies and the Americas is bittersweet. The sweet part is that Moravian missionaries defended the humanity of slaves as soul-bearing men and women made in God's image. In an age where slaves were considered soulless tools to be used and discarded, the Moravian mission affirmed the dignity of the African. Many of the African converts were given responsibilities in the mission. In essence they became small group leaders, meeting regularly and overseeing the spiritual health of a group of five or more other believers. Some of the early black preachers were converts from Moravian missionary work. In the early days of the Pennsylvania and North Carolina Moravian settlements, African American slaves lived in almost every respect like their white brothers and sisters, worshiping, working and serving in an integrated community: "Here black and white Brethren washed each other's feet in wooden tubs. Here—albeit for different reasons—they groped toward the chance that a common faith would replace the whip as the currency of interracial discourse." Naturally, plantation owners in the beginning were quite resistant to Moravian work and openly hindered the missionaries, at times trumping up charges to imprison them. They were afraid that the gospel message would inspire a slave rebellion by sowing dangerous notions of equality. In addition, the Moravians' high view of slaves earned them a low view in the eyes of the Church of England clergy in the West Indies who believed that Christianity was for whites only, and "saw the Moravians as obnoxious intruders."

The "bitter" part of their work among slaves was that within the Moravian community, slaves were still slaves. Moravians believed that a person was to accept whatever station of life he or she was born into, and despite their ability to stand up for religious freedom, they did not contest the social stratifications of their day. To their credit, they lived what they preached. If a Moravian was born on the bottom rung, they did not think social advancement something they should pursue. Aristocracy like Zinzendorf embraced his station in life as a nobleman just like Anna's father did as a laborer. Before God there was equality, but before humans there was not, and that was that. Therefore, Moravians not only accepted slavery, they also succumbed to the purchase of slaves. And though some slaves have written generously about their community life with the Moravians, the fact that they were differentiated based on skin color is an abomination just the same. However, later Moravians expressed remorse over this belief and practice. Lloyd Cook, Jamaican historian and lecturer at Jamaica Bible College, writes,

> I do not think that we should fault the Moravians too much for their involve-

ment in slavery. They have expressed publicly their regret of their former complicity: an unintended one. Here in Jamaica they did cease their operating an estate in 1824. Writers of their Jamaican history have publicly repudiated this early involvement. They were strong advocates for the slaves, even during the time of their complicity with slavery, and certainly only did get involved out of the need to support themselves financially on the fields, as there was no other arrangement for their support.

When you're living on the fringe, things look differently.

GETTING PERSPECTIVE

The Moravians, like the new friars, were broken people living on the broken edges of a broken world. They suffered, served and at times unintentionally played into the systems that kept certain people on the outside. It was an occupational hazard of loving people on the margins of society—one that the new friars, no doubt, will face. It's so easy for those of us in the mainstream to judge those in ministry on the margins. But when you're living on the fringe, things look differently. "How can you expect a man who's warm to understand a man who's cold?" writes Solzhenitsyn about a man living in a Siberian work camp in his book *One Day in the Life of Ivan Denisovich.* The new friar communities in the margins are making decisions as best they can from their view of things from where they live at the edge of the world. We will need to allow them the privilege of victory and set back as they fuse themselves to the people who live in the wake of the disaster we call the twentieth century.

T he darkest hours of the night are the ones just before dawn, when it seems as if the sun has been swallowed by darkness and there are no signs of it ever returning. So it has been with each of the movements of friars. Their arrival occurred at the very nadir of the church or of civilization itself, when hope was lowest and evil appeared to have the day. The Celtic monastic movement was birthed at what must have felt to some like the end of the Roman Empire, and it was so profoundly regenerative that one author suggests that the Celtic monastic movement saved civilization! And the Jesuits showed up at a time when the papacy had sunk to new lows—politically and morally. Fifty years before the order was founded, Pope Innocent III awarded a cardinalship to thirteen-year-old Giovanni de' Medici as a favor to wealthy friends, and immorality was so widespread among bishops and priests that many were known to have sired children and given them prominent clerical posts. In Francis's time the crusades had polarized the East and West, and the nobility and clergy were hopelessly out of touch with the masses of peasants. What's more, the forces of religious oppression and persecution were the very things that brought to life the Moravian and the Nestorian movements. Each of the mission-driven orders mentioned in this book appeared at some of the grimmest moments for the human family. It is the way of God. When his creation has brought upon itself new levels of degradation, he shows up through a fresh move of his Spirit, bringing new levels of elevation at the hands of men and women devoted to his kingdom purposes.

We occupy such an infinitesimal speck on a big planet for just a few nanoseconds of human history. I've read very little of all that's out there on human history; I can't even remember what I had for dinner last night much less give any real sense of how the last hundred years compare with any other time in history. So it's quite audacious of me to say that life on this side of the twentieth century is worse than at any other time in the whole of our life on earth. I say it with a little humility, recognizing that there have been many wonderful advances in the last hundred years to make life easier for a great many people, and granting the possibility that I am dead wrong—but still I would suggest that life on earth has never been nastier than it is right now. The second law of thermodynamics says that things in nature move from order to disorder, and it seems to be happening with human history too. If ever we needed passionately dedicated and intimately devout communities of missional monks and nuns, it is now.

Life on earth has certainly had its harsh realities from age to age. To have a Celtic horde come sweeping through your village, or to live in the midst of the Black Plague, or to be captured as a slave and survive the journey to a new world only to live a life of hard labor in the West Indies must have been simply awful. And no one would deny that life before the world had flush toilets was a pretty smelly ordeal! But I believe there are at least five reasons why the twentieth century was an unmitigated disaster: the globalization of poverty, the destruction of the environment, the neglect and exploitation of children, runaway urbanization, and the scale of our self-destruction. These five factors have made life harder for more people than it's ever been since the dawn of humanity, and they point to the dire necessity for a wave of new friars who vow themselves in the name of Jesus to a life of justice and holiness—men and women willing to descend the walls of intractable poverty in order to restore dignity and usher in the kingdom of God to those living and dying on the margins.

THE GLOBALIZATION OF POVERTY

Many of the push forces of intractable poverty mentioned in chapter two emerged in the twentieth century. Michel Chossudovsky, professor of economics at the University of Ottawa in Canada and author of *The Globalisation of Poverty: Impacts of IMF and World Bank Reforms,* states, "The late 20th Century will go down in world history as a period of global impoverishment marked by the collapse of productive systems in the developing world, the demise of national institutions and the disintegration of health and educational programmes." One reason Chossudovsky believes that the late twentieth century was such an economic disaster is that during this period unemployment went global. When the world has 200 million surplus laborers in China, the price of a day's labor in the rest of the world is depressed as a result. Those of us who live in the insular womb of the West have very little idea what a world where half of the workforce can't earn enough money to keep themselves or their families out of desperate poverty looks like. Those who are old enough to have lived through the Great Depression in America have a better idea than most. They only have to trace the trajectory of the Great Depression out a few decades to envisage what our country might look like under the chronic unemployment experienced by so many countries in the developing world. Walk into any corrugated-tin slum community and you will begin to appreciate the effects of the globalized labor crisis and the volume of poverty in our world.

Even taking into consideration the horrific growth in the gap between rich and poor mentioned earlier, you might argue that this does not prove that the desperation of the poor in the twenty-first century is any worse than the desperation of the poor in any other century. Perhaps not, but you should at least grant me that there are *quantitatively* more dreadfully poor people on our planet than ever before with 2.7 billion people now living below \$2 U.S. per day. Some of this poverty is quite concentrated. For instance, 97 percent of Uganda and 73 percent of Tanzania live in this kind of intractable poverty. And I would argue that the poverty of the hunter-gatherer or even the feudal peasant in pre-industrial times was qualitatively better than the poverty of the urban slum-dweller.

THE DESTRUCTION OF THE ENVIRONMENT

It doesn't take a rocket scientist to ascertain that the planet is showing signs of wear. I suppose that's to be expected given how many miles we've put on the environmental odometer. We began the twentieth century with 1.6 billion inhabitants and ended it with 6.1 billion. To grow the first billion earthlings took a really, really long time—centuries . . . millennia . . . Now a billion new earth-dwellers get added every ten years or so. Adding so many people in such a short time has taken its toll. The twentieth century has easily been harder on our environment than any other.

Don't get me wrong, many great advances have been made as well. We are yielding larger harvests with less soil, we've figured out how to use the elements of our earth to cure many pernicious diseases that have plagued our race, and we have started to explore ways to harness solar energy to run our hair dryers. (Of course, we could just stand outside in the sun.) We know more than we ever have about how this planet works, and about the creatures that share it with us. But somewhere in the twentieth century a few steps forward were offset by several gigantic steps backward.

The last couple of centuries have witnessed the greatest extinction of species since the dinosaurs. Over the past 500 years, 128 species of birds have vanished; 103 of those have disappeared since 1800. At no other time on God's good earth have so many people (three billion to be exact) lacked adequate means to dispose of their feces, creating incredible biological haz-

**We are using up our planet,
and the world's poor are feeling it most.**

ards. We are spitting pollutants into the air, water and soil like never before, forests are disappearing while deserts are encroaching on fertile land, there's a hole in the ozone, and we can't dig landfills quickly enough to dispose of all the Styrofoam cups and baby diapers we keep going through. If the entire planet lived like North Americans, we'd need two more earths just to keep the supply of lattes, Lexuses and other luxury items flowing in order to accommodate our voracious environmental appetite. We are using up our planet, and the world's poor are feeling it most.

Dr. Chester Wood, dean of doctoral studies of Nairobi Evangelical Graduate School of Theology, relates a story from his days in the Philippines. Apparently a small coastal village was suffering under debilitating poverty. A development organization began to work with leaders in the village to establish a fishery. In time, the economic benefits of the fishery began to breathe new life into the little village. The standard of living grew for everyone and fewer residents suffered the intractable poverty they had once known. Then one day, a Japanese factory opened up nearby and began dumping their byproducts into the ocean. Within a short time the fish in the fishery died and the booming business folded. The village returned to its former state of impoverishment and the Japanese factory no doubt found a fresh influx of cheap labor from the residents. "The field of the poor may yield much food," Proverbs 13:23 says, "but it is swept away through injustice."

The poor are the most vulnerable people in the world. When something goes wrong with the environment, the poor tend to be the first to reap the consequences. That's not to say that the poor don't do their fair share of harming the environment. In their desperation, people living on the edge of survival certainly contribute to environmental problems. Feeding their kids comes before conservation, so the poor often overuse the resources around them, depleting the soil of nutrients by overfarming or destroying marine environments by overfishing. But the reality is that the poor suffer most when the earth suffers, and the earth is in bad shape at the moment.

THE NEGLECT AND EXPLOITATION OF CHILDREN

The rise of street kids and single-parent homes worldwide, the booming sex-slave trade, the number of children being abducted and trained to kill, forty-six million abortions every year, fifteen million children orphaned by AIDS—these are signs of a social disintegration happening at the most fundamental level all around the world. The nuclear family is the essential building block of society, and it is in as bad of shape globally as it has ever been. At various times and in various locations the family has suffered set-backs, but at no other time have so many families been so ravaged by so many different forces.

AIDS in Africa and increasingly in Asia is leaving a generation of house-holds headed by kids. The extended family structure is not able to accommodate the number of children left motherless and fatherless by the pandemic. Some parents with AIDS pray actively that their HIV-positive children will die first so that they will not have to face the hardship of providing for their brothers or sisters. Who will care for these orphans whose extended family structure has come unraveled?

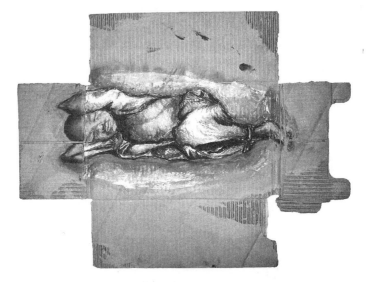

The Color of My Neglect, **by Grace Smith**

What about all the kids who live in bus depots or under bridges or in train stations? Some are orphans; others have parents who have stopped caring about their own lives let alone the lives of their kids. Consider Ricardo, who lives on the streets of Montevideo, Uruguay. Ricardo told his story to

Jenny Smith, freelance writer for *New Internationalist*.

I am 16, but not for much longer. My birthday is in January, although I have never received a birthday present in my life. I've been living on the street for the last six years. . . .

In the morning I wake up and wash my face—in the fountain if I sleep in the plaza or outside the cinema, and in the sea if I sleep in the bathroom. Then I work till 4 pm and after that I buy milanesa [meat coated in breadcrumbs], drink wine and smoke marijuana. If I am drunk, I like to go to the beach. I drink and smoke marijuana often but only take pastabase occasionally [a form of crack cocaine, highly addictive and very cheap] because I only wish to try it. I don't like it because it makes me crazy. I buy it from a house, from a man who sells to us children. I can give you the address and phone number if you like. [Dealers invite children into their homes with offers of food in order to get them hooked.] I smoke and drink because I need to forget my day—my situation, my life, is difficult and I need help to sleep.

Ricardo has been raped and has spent time in jail; he has friends who have been killed. The life Ricardo lives is beyond my comprehension. The number of kids who live on the streets is also beyond my comprehension—over 100 million. Since the global population of those under the age of fifteen is 1.8 billion, that means one out of every twenty kids on earth lives on the streets. Has a tragedy of this proportion ever been visited upon children in any other era? Kids have suffered in every age, but I doubt that such a high

> **One out of every twenty kids on earth lives on the streets.**

percentage of the world's children have lived without the supervision of a responsible adult. The book *Lord of the Flies* has come true, only instead of an island setting, the children live in an urban jungle and are subject to the unrestrained abuse of adults who know they can do whatever they want to street kids and no one will care.

Simultaneous to a rise in the world's children being turned out onto the streets is a rise in the world's children being sold into sexual slavery. Prostitution may be the oldest profession in the world, but at no other time have so many children been sold—many by their parents—into the sex-slave trade. At the start of the twenty-first century, nearly two million children were involved in the sex industry. Jocasta Shakespeare writes:

> Her eyes are made up heavily with black kohl, lips reddened and fingernails lacquered pink. But no amount of make-up can disguise the child-size feet in tiny red flip-flops, the pre-pubescent figure hidden under a sailor-collared shirt or the high-pitched voice. "My father sold me for 200 baht ($5) two months ago," she says. "He comes to the brothel every month to collect 3000 baht ($75) from Big Ma. I clean Big Ma's house in the day and then work as a prostitute at night. I don't get money at all—just food. I get one man a night but most of the girls go with six or seven men a night." Kok says she has never used a condom.

The recent boom in the underage sex trade, with an estimated 800,000 children currently working as prostitutes in Thailand, is partly due to the mistaken belief that children are too young to contract AIDS. On the contrary, immature bodies unready for sex tear easily and are especially vulnerable to infections. Most prostitutes wear nothing but a little Buddhist charm folded into their bra straps for protection against disease.

The ugly reality faced by so many hundreds of thousands of boys and girls who serve as sex toys is surely a sign that we have reached new levels of savagery and social disintegration. Add to this the horrors children face in war and the picture is even more bleak. There is an African saying, "When the elephants fight, the grass gets trampled." Children are the primary victims of war since they are often a society's most vulnerable demographic. The technology to create smaller and lighter assault weapons has meant that we can arm children with deadly guns. A man named Frank who I met the other day told me about his experience with a four-year-old girl while he was fighting in Vietnam. At one point he began to babble and cry. "I had to kill her," he kept saying. He composed himself and related the awful story. Apparently a small Vietnamese child was sent into Frank's company with a backpack of explosives strapped to her back as a little obedient walking bomb. Frank kept shouting and begging her to stop but she just kept replying, "I'm coming Joe. I'm coming." Frank shot and killed her and has suffered alcoholism and depression for years since. Today the number of children being used in armed conflict probably runs in the hundreds of thousands. It is a sorry population that makes its children fight their wars.

RUNAWAY URBANIZATION

In 1920, three out of four urbanites lived in Europe and North America while the rest of the world lived a rural life. But as the colonial machine wound down and mechanization wound up something started to happen: millions upon millions of villagers put their few belongings on a cart and moved to the city, creating the most dramatic movement of people the earth has ever witnessed. During the twentieth century, city dwellers increased twentyfold, with most of that growth occurring in the developing world, overwhelming urban infrastructures. It happened, in part, because money began puddling up into fewer pools and land became concentrated in the hands of fewer but larger operations. Private and corporate landowners turned many little plots once used to feed a rural population into giant cash crop farms that produced things like sugar and coffee. Not many rural peasants could get jobs working for these mega-operations because agriculture became mechanized, and what once required a team of fifty laborers could now be done by one man and a machine. At the same time, factories were popping up in cities and the call for unskilled labor was wooing unemployed village farmers. Young people, eager to throw off the shackles of rural cultural restraints, also found the call to the city irresistible. Without warning, cities in the postcolonial world whose populations had been more or less constant or growing very slowly began to double and triple in size. The governments put in place by the departing colonial powers were brand new. Some were dictatorships, others fledgling democracies, but none were prepared for rapid urbanization. The Americans, British and French did not leave instructions on what to do when a capital city triples in size. How could governments collect the garbage and build houses and create jobs and handle the increased inner-city transportation load under such swift growth? The short answer is that they couldn't, and city infrastructures buckled under the stress. But the human creature is amazingly adaptable, resourceful and resilient, so the urban slum community was born to fill the gap.

Metro Manila grew from 2.5 million in 1964 to over 12 million in 2000

Most of us who grew up in a suburban neighborhood will need to use our imaginations to appreciate what life for over one billion slum-dwellers is like. Try to picture the neighborhood of two hundred families in which you grew up razed by a natural disaster. Everything in your home has been lost. The disaster was of such magnitude that your land is now worthless, all the insurance companies have folded, your parents have lost their jobs, and the bank had to sell your property. Everyone you know is in a similar situation. You and your neighbors will have to make do.

Remarkably, your family's garden shed was left standing. You and your parents and siblings relocate the shed to a nearby drainage ditch (which will now serve as a public toilet) and move in. Most of your neighbors do the same. One of your aunts with her three kids is in even worse shape, so your dad invites them to live with you all in the shed. An industrious neighbor bravely attaches a cable from the power lines overhead and runs it into his shed. In no time at all your whole community, which swelled to four hundred families overnight due to the migration of relatives like your aunt, has electric power.

Very quickly you learn that there are two ways to get money: selling drugs or selling your body. Luckily your dad manages to get a job mowing the lawn of the one rich family living in a nearby mansion for a few dollars an hour (they're the ones who bought your property from the bank for next to nothing). He gets you and your sister a job cleaning the house. Your mom and the others in your household buy Hostess Twinkies, Ding Dongs and Cup Cakes and sell them to passersby on a busy street at a profit of about fifty cents each. Stretch this scenario out a few generations, multiplying the number in your neighborhood every few years, and you are beginning to imagine life in a slum community.

It's not all bad. Neighbors who were just acquaintances in the suburban reality are now like family. There's no privacy anyway, and with everybody living on top of each other in the same miserable conditions you can't help but build many close friendships (along with a couple of "choice" neighbors whom you can't stand). By and large you have a real community. However, there is enough sickness, despair, stress and hardship that life takes on a grinding quality. Dignity dies and soon you just stop caring. It is this urban version of impoverishment that is new to humanity and that gives a qualitatively different dimension to poverty in the twenty-first century.

THE SCALE OF OUR SELF-DESTRUCTION

After millennia of practice, humans have gotten quite good at killing one another. Systematic annihilation has always existed; it's just that our systems have gotten more efficient. In fact, in the twentieth century alone we managed to kill more people than in all the other centuries combined. Quite an accomplishment when you consider that the century began with the war that was going to end all wars. By 1944 we had to invent a word to describe a particular kind of killing that had reached new levels in its scope of destruction: *genocide*. This form of killing is more than just the run-of-the-mill petty commander trying to exterminate an enemy ethnic group. Genocide is the systematic and planned extermination of an entire group of people from earth. The Armenian genocide, the Nazi Holocaust, Stalin's forced famine, Pol Pot's killing fields, the Rwandan genocide—these are the most famous. There were many, many more systematic human extermination campaigns in the twentieth century.

Alfred Nobel said, "The day that two army corps can annihilate one another in one second, the civilized nations will shrink from war and discharge their troops." Unfortunately this has not been the case. The introduction of chemical and nuclear warfare did not deter us from making war but instead has increased the scale of our destruction. Since 1990 civil wars have far outpaced interstate wars in the number of ongoing conflicts. While these wars do not match the World Wars in the number of casualties, the global, aggregate scale of destruction due to armed conflict today is unacceptably high. One researcher estimates that nearly 100 million deaths resulted from twentieth-century wars—six times the number of war-related deaths of the eighteenth and nineteenth centuries combined. Of course, the hardest hit by war are the vulnerable populations—the poor, the children, the elderly, sick and dying. It is upon them that the greatest burden of a war-torn century has rested.

DEATH COMES BEFORE RESURRECTION

Morris Berman, in his book *The Twilight of American Culture,* says that collapse is built into the process of civilization. Berman is convinced we are in the final stages of decline within Western civilization, using clever phrases like the "Coca-colonization of the planet," the " 'Rambification' of entertainment" and the "moronization of the American public." He suggests that we have one hundred to two hundred years of decline left (perhaps punctuated with a burst of renaissance) before we see the final puff of smoke from the flickering candle. Berman calls for new monastic individuals to take up the mantle of preserving all that is good and right and true about us and our history before it completely disappears from the planet.

While much of what Berman says about the decay of American culture is spot on, his description of the new monastic individual feels to me like it comes out of humanistic academia rather than a deeply spiritual sense that God loves the world and is calling his people to incarnate the gospel to those on the edges. What I am seeing is that men and women, possessed of a holy compulsion to love the unlovely, are beginning to bind their destinies to those who live under the boot of unjust power structures. They have cast their lot with the poor and have embraced marginalization in the name of breathing hope into despair. Whether the systems of thought and life and culture as we know it in the West prevail or fail, the new friars have begun to move into slum communities around the world, and they will not leave until they see the kingdom of God firmly established.

CONCLUSION

In Mark 10, Jesus started off on his final trip—one that would cost him everything. He was heading to Jerusalem, where he would be made into a spectacle and publicly humiliated. He'd be openly tried, beaten quite severely, stripped naked and crucified, and it would all be turned into a form of entertainment for the amusement-starved, circus-loving crowds at the eastern edge of the Roman Empire. Worse yet, those who had pledged their love to him would scatter like cockroaches when the lights came on. Jesus was about to be drained of the few things he possessed: his life, his earthly friendships and an unspeakably intimate fellowship with the Father—a Father who was about to ask his Son to voluntarily accept the ugliness of every rape, murder and lie. Jesus would say yes to him, and it would result in his death and in his estrangement from his *Abba,* his Daddy.

At this stage in the disciples' two- to three-year friendship with Jesus, they knew something of the cost of following him. Peter reminds Jesus in Mark 10 that they had left every worldly thing to follow this young Rabbi. In that same chapter, Mark tells of another young man who wanted to know what eternal life would cost him. He was what Americans in the 1980s called a yuppie, and very likely looked the part. Probably twenty-something. A youth who had likely amassed his wealth the way many twenty-something millionaires today do: they are born into a state of privilege, and they leverage their contacts with others of privilege as well as their access to resources in order to grow their wealth rapidly. There are very few who can accumulate a large portfolio while still in their twenties without using papa's money, friendships with other rich people and perhaps the inevitable stepping on a few heads on the way up the ladder. How did this young man come by his wealth? We are not told. We only know that he did not earn the money through a lifetime of hard work and saving.

The man ran up, interrupting their ragamuffin caravan, and knelt down in front of Jesus. "Good Teacher," he said. "What must I do to get eternal life?" Jesus saw something in his use of the phrase "good teacher" that I don't fully understand. Cultural anthropologist Bruce Malina says that in a society like first-century Palestine's, "good" was a limited commodity, and this young man was issuing a subtle suggestion that Jesus acquired his position of "good" teacher at the expense of others. Or maybe it was simply the sort of thing that happens when a person of worldly status addresses a person of religious status. It's like saying, "Even though I control vast worldly resources and use people to get what I want, I'm really one of you holy guys. See how reverently I seek out your wisdom." Perhaps it was this rich kid's desire to appear righteous, a little like a mob boss kissing the ring of the pope. Whatever it was, Jesus called into question his use of the term *good*. "Why do you call me good?" Jesus asked. "God is the only one who is really and truly good." Some commentators suggest that this statement is another claim Jesus was laying to deity. Maybe. Or maybe Jesus saw in this man's fragile soul a feigned respect that was not backed up by a willingness to honor Jesus with something more than words. Maybe Jesus was saying, "Why are you calling me good with your mouth when you life reveals that you really don't think I'm all that good?"

Whatever the case, Jesus moves from questioning the young man's use of the word *good* to choosing a handful of biblical commands that might define piety to a first-century Jew concerned with outward appearance: "You know the commandments: 'Do not murder. Do not commit adultery. Do not steal. Do not testify falsely. Do not cheat. Honor your father and mother.' " Interestingly, Jesus leaves out the command that he previously had told one lawyer was the greatest commandment—to love God with all your heart, soul, mind and strength. It was as if Jesus could see that this man's love for the "technical" forms of piety had become null and void because it was not inspired by a pure and true love for God. Jesus wanted to temporarily reinforce the external piety so that he could take him one step deeper. So when the young man professed to have faithfully kept these commands since childhood, Jesus didn't bring out his "Sermon on the Mount" speech. That would have been an obvious response to the man's claim that he hadn't slipped up on any of the particular commands that Jesus listed. Jesus could have hit him where he lived by making him look at the difference between keeping the outward appearance of the law versus obeying the inward spirit of the law. He could have talked about lust really being a form of adultery and hatred being counted as murder in God's eyes—things the rich young ruler would have had to concede that he hadn't kept.

Instead, Mark says that Jesus looked at him and welled up with love for him. What was it Jesus saw that stirred his love for this rich young man? Could he see that deep under the layers of bondage to material possessions was a person who yearned to live free from the intoxicating love of money? Jesus said that there was only one thing left that he hadn't done that stood between him and eternal life: to liquidate all his assets and give the money to the poor. "Then come, follow me," Jesus invited him, "and you will have treasure in heaven."

> **The amassing of treasure isn't bad,
> just the type of treasure and where it's located.**

The amassing of treasure isn't bad, just the type of treasure and where it's located. One of the things I love about Francis is that he never disparaged the rich. They were precious to God and therefore precious to Francis. I have met many poor people who are more materialistic than rich people I know. And while many of the new friars have managed to free themselves from the pursuit of wealth, they struggle with many other less obvious idols, such as the worship of Christ's mission, spiritual pride or humanistic idealism.

Dietrich Bonhoeffer said, "When Christ calls a man, he bids him come and die." Jesus is the only worthy obsession; all other obsessions must be beaten into submission. The first test of this rich young ruler was to see if he could subjugate the wealth he had been given to the prospect of following Jesus on his way to the cross, without holding any of it back "just in case." It is one of the very first tests of discipleship, and it was a call that this money-addict was unable or unwilling to muster the strength to obey. Jesus' plea for him to leave his possessions brought on a sense of gloom for the man. He left depressed, knowing his obsession with money had captured his heart. He turned away with sadness because he knew he was choosing money over life itself.

MONEY-FREE

It is this story of the rich young ruler that rattles the bank accounts of a handful of men and women throughout history who took Jesus at his word, sold everything they had, gave it to the poor and embarked with him into a possession-deprived existence: Patrick, Brigid, Francis, Clare, Bar Sauma and countless others through time. God seems to be quite happy to raise up key people of wealth and call them to give it all up in order to bind themselves and their future to the poor and oppressed. These key men and women are looking ahead to something that is more delicious than an extravagant meal and more luxurious than any treasure of earth. They want more. I suppose you could say

> **The universal call, to any who profess to follow Jesus, is to believe that he is the Son of God and to act like it, no matter what we do for a living.**

they are greedy—greedy for freedom. Deeply unsatisfied with wealth, they crave something more than the freedom that comes from owning many possessions. Instead of the freedom of private ownership they want freedom *from* private ownership and the chains that come with it. Proverbs 16:19 says, "It is better to be of a lowly spirit among the poor / than to divide the spoil with the proud." People like this tend to show up when the church is drunk with power and in a state of decline. They spawn an era of new growth among the marginalized and renewal among the mainstream. They gain a small but devout following, and their influence spreads widely. I believe we are at the front edge of just such a time.

The call of the friars to bind themselves to the poor in a vocational way is a particular call, not a universal one. The universal call to any who profess to follow Jesus is to believe that he is the Son of God and to act like it, no matter what we do for a living. And while the qualities that are emerging among new friar communities seem radical, they are ones all of us would do well to embrace:

- incarnation—tearing down the insulation and becoming real to those in trouble
- devotion—making intimacy with Christ our all-consuming passion
- community—intentionally creating interdependence with others
- mission—looking outside ourselves
- marginalization—being countercultural in a world that beckons us to assimilate at the cost of our conscience

In the Old Testament King David made an ordinance whereby everyone shared in the plunder of the enemy whether they went into battle or not (1 Samuel 30:23-25). The glory of victory was reserved not only for those who fought in the trenches but also for those who stayed behind to guard the supplies and keep the Israelite towns functioning. Not everyone is called to the missional vocation of a new friar, but that doesn't mean the men and women taking up residence among those trapped in poverty and despair have to be alone in their work. Francis encouraged what he called a third order. The first order was the Franciscan men, the second was the Poor Clares, and the third was made up of men and women living sacrificially and simply in the work-a-day world while supporting and praying for the first two orders. This was not, in any way, designed to create a spiritual hierarchy (first-place winners are the Franciscan men, the women following Clare are second, and third place goes to the losers who didn't qualify for the other two). In creating a third order, Francis was acknowledging that while a few were called to the Franciscan and Poor Clare orders, many were called to embrace their values.

Over the next fifty to one hundred years (should humanity last that long), I believe we'll see full-fledged twenty-first-century manifestations of these old orders among the poor—movements like the Franciscans or the radical missionaries of the Celtic and Nestorian monks, new friars, slum-dwelling Nazirites, communities like the Jesuits and the Moravians, bent on living a devoted life together on the fringe of the global empire. They may not don the robes or cut the tonsure into their hair. They may instead have pierced body parts or tattoos that bear some symbolic significance to their commitment. They may live on the streets with the homeless or in slum communities with the dispossessed. They may lack the austerity of the old orders, but they embody the radical spirit that possessed the monks and nuns of old, many of whom turned their backs on wealth and opportunity in order to count themselves among the oppressed and to obtain something better than wealth: communion with God and a taste of his kingdom on earth.

AFTERWORD

Darkest Night of the Year
Heather Coaster, serving with Word Made Flesh (WMF) in Bolivia

Darkest Night of the Year." It's the title of Over the Rhine's Christmas album, but the words themselves seem to be the mantra to which I walk as I pass in and out of brothel doors. For all the times I've entered these places, let my eyes adjust to the dim red glow of the interior, tried to block out the mixed smell of alcohol, sex and urine, swallowed the never-dulling shock and disgust of passing an exiting client as I make my way toward one of my friends, tonight somehow feels different, darker in a way that didn't seem possible before.

I spent the earlier part of the day baking cookies, searching El Alto's market for wrapping paper, and reading e-mails that brought Christmas greetings from home and with them tears for the reminders of family and friends with whom I wasn't. Now I clutch my paper scribbled with newly learned Christmas carols in Spanish and follow this ridiculous looking group of WMF Bolivia staff and volunteers, sporting Santa hats, a guitar and recorder for accompaniment, a thermos full of hot chocolate, and a supply of plastic Dixie cups. We have been told the girls working tonight will be few, but find more than we expect. I am not the only one away from family tonight. I make eye contact with one of the men and wonder who might be missing him this *Noche Buena* (Christmas Eve). The music is loud, the request for temporary reprieve is granted, and we find ourselves in a suddenly silent brothel, under the gazes of clients and girls.

To the tune of Silent Night we sing, *"Noche de amor, noche de paz."* Night of love, night of peace. It feels almost mocking. How can I sing of love and peace in this place where the most beautiful expressions of love are defiled, where peace is shattered repeatedly? I make my way to one of the girls in a doorway.

I don't know her well, can't remember her name, but recognize her from lunches at the center. I receive a warm look of recognition from her as well, greet her with a customary kiss, embrace and find her falling into me, the jerk of a sob on my shoulder. She holds me for a moment, then pulls away, wipes her tears, and I take her hand and lead her to where the rest of the group has gathered, pulling the song sheet from my pocket. I stand there with my hand over her shoulder, fingers intertwined in hers and hear her voice join our little indiscriminate choir. *O santa noche.* How can this night be holy?

But these are the songs we sing, about silent, holy nights of love and peace. A night both dark and sacred. Quiet enough to crave the cry of a baby king, black enough to welcome the light of the star of Bethlehem. *The Darkest Night of the Year.* And into this night we are asked to bring Truth. Say to Daughter Zion, "See, your Savior comes" (Isaiah 62:11). We are asked to carry light, to hold the hand of one of his beloved, to tell her she is remembered.

It is later, back at the center, as the guitar is being packed up and hats are coming off. Humberto, our friend and board director will describe this night as the most *atrevido* of his life. *Atrevido.* This one word holds implications of boldness, insolence, daring. And perhaps it is. Perhaps this is indeed the scandal of the gospel. And perhaps tonight I understand it in a way that I never have before.

With tears in my own eyes, I had asked her to come with us. Begged her to leave. She stayed. We had continued on, singing those same carols a dozen times more, receiving skeptical looks from bouncers and applause from drunken men. The girls were quieter recipients, but in the weeks that followed we would hear *gracias* a hundred times or more. Thank you. Thank you for remembering us.

And he does. He remembers her. He comes *for* her, *to* her, into the darkest of nights, into her darkest of rooms. He stands with her there and holds her hand.

See, your Savior comes.

"It gets darker and darker, and then Jesus is born."
Wendell Berry

APPENDIX A

HOW TO JOIN THE NEW FRIARS

The organizations mentioned in this book and listed below have "on ramps" that people can travel upon for a short period of time in order to explore a life of service among the poor. Before journeying onto one of these ramps, here are some helpful questions to ask:

1. Would people around me describe me as teachable, flexible and passionate about Jesus?

2. Are there ways that my life today exhibits a practical love for the poor?

3. Can those who know me best confirm a call to love and serve those living in desperate conditions?

If there is a conviction within your community that you should explore becoming a servant to the poor through a community that lives incarnationally among the poor, then check out the following organizations and opportunities.

InnerCHANGE

www.innerchange.org

InnerCHANGE is a Christian order composed of communities of missionaries living and ministering incarnationally among the poor and striving to follow the Lord God's injunction to "act justly and to love mercy and to walk humbly with your God" (Micah 6:8 NIV).

"What we do is substantially different from most mission agencies," says John Hayes, who planted himself among the poor in Santa Ana, California, in 1985. "Most agencies working incarnationally among the poor experience a high degree of burnout. Our impulse to become an order was to create a structure among the poor that people could join for long seasons, even a lifetime, and thrive." Apparently it's working; InnerCHANGE has very little turnover. Those who join this order tend to stay, even though they are living in some of the most intense urban poverty this world has to offer.

InnerCHANGE communities currently exist in Los Angeles and San Francisco, California; Minneapolis, Minnesota; Caracas, Venezuela; Iasi, Romania; and Phnom Penh and Kampong, Cambodia. InnerCHANGE offers internships of less than a year as well as year-long apprenticeships. There are helpful descriptions of what "a day in the life" looks like for their interns, as well as brief descriptions of their programs at their website.

SERVANT PARTNERS

www.servantpartners.org

In 1992 Tom Pratt, then an InterVarsity urban project director, gathered a small group to discuss and pray about some of the prophetic challenges that people like John Perkins and Viv Grigg were laying out for the Western church. That next year Tom founded Servant Partners with a call to become a global mission serving the urban poor in squatter communities in megacities around the world. In the last three years sixty young people have joined this holistic church-planting mission with many others now in the "pipeline." Servant Partners' sites include Bangkok, Thailand; Mexico City, Mexico; Manila, Philippines; and other locations including cities in the Middle East and North Africa.

Servant Partners offers two short-term opportunities to help people discern God's call on their life. One is a two-year internship based in L.A. with a month-long stint in Manila. The other is an international internship of varying lengths held in Manila and shaped by the intern.

SERVANTS TO ASIA'S URBAN POOR

www.servantsasia.org

Servants to Asia's Urban Poor (Servants) is an order that was set up in the early 1980s by Viv Grigg, based out of his home country of New Zealand. Servants workers come from all over the world and are now living incarnationally and ministering to the urban poor in slum communities in Indonesia, India, the Philippines and Cambodia. New Servants teams are being raised up to go to East Timor and Myanmar. Their strategy involves a good deal of networking. "We will build relationships with other people and groups involved in ministry among the poor and we will work with churches of all denominations [that] are happy to partner with us. We will promote the needs and aspirations of the poor among the middle class and rich with the aim of seeing them mobilized to participate with the poor, both in field and home countries."

Servants has a great online discussion forum on their website so that you can interact with the curious and the serious on matters of urban poverty and compassionate service. The "Steps to Joining" page includes a listing of the various service opportunities and check out their five-phase process to becoming a Servants team member.

URBAN NEIGHBOURS OF HOPE

www.unoh.org

The seeds of Urban Neighbours of Hope (UNOH) sprang from the combustible mixture of an international ministry to young people (Australia's Youth for Christ movement) and a network of independent Christian churches (the Churches of Christ). Ash and Anji Barker founded a community among the poor in Springvale, Australia, a multicultural settlement in Melbourne. John Hayes of InnerCHANGE, along with a New Zealand Youth for Christ leader named Daryl Gardiner, assisted UNOH in defining itself as an order. InnerCHANGE and UNOH have formed the Gospel Order Alliance, which aims to "help nurture the emergence of a new wave of orders and work collaboratively to reach the urban poor." More about UNOH and their vision can be obtained from Ash Barker's book *Surrender All: A Call to Sub-merge with Christ* (Springvale, Australia: Urban Neighbours of Hope Publications, 2005).

UNOH has a nine-day or a one-month training program if you live in the greater Melbourne (Victoria, Australia) area and want to explore what it might mean to join their order. For those wanting a more thorough examination of life as a UNOH missionary, there are one- and two-year programs. Check out the "What We Do" link at their website.

WORD MADE FLESH

www.wordmadeflesh.com

Beginning in 1994 in Chennai (Madras), India, Chris Heuertz, his wife, Phileena, and six or seven others sought simply to serve Christ, one another and the poor—in that order. Heuertz says that they've never really had any sort of emphasis on recruiting. Nonetheless, Word Made Flesh (WMF) has exploded. Today they have more than 130 staff and board members and have sent more than 500 short-termers to serve in 12 cities in 11 countries. "We do not view growth as a sign of success," he admits. For the men and women in WMF, their love of Christ and their communion with one another come before growth. WMF missionary Daphne Eck writes of the early days, "We were a fledgling organization comprised of a few kids with spanking new bachelor's degrees and passion for Jesus and the poor. We recklessly jumped into a life that most of our parents, friends and churches didn't think possible or logical. . . . We have experienced growth beyond our years, not only in our numbers, but also in our spirituality and as leaders in mission among the poor."

WMF organizes four-month Servant Teams to many of the locations where their communities serve. Four to seven individuals will commit themselves to service and discipleship under the leadership of a WMF missionary. Learn more about the Servant Teams at their website.

STILL IN SCHOOL?

Most of these fellowships want you to at least finish high school and some may want you to go through college before you join them. If you are in college and want to take a next step, consider coming to one of the Urbana Student Mission Conventions held every three years from December 27-31 (2006, 2009, 2012 . . .). The Urbana website (<www.urbana.org>) has a large database of excellent articles and resources for college students considering a career in missions.

If you are a college student and would like to go on a summer program, check out the Global Urban Trek at <www.urbana.org/feat.trek.home.cfm>. This program is designed to help students discern God's call to become a new friar by placing them in a living and serving context alongside the poor in some of the world's slum communities.

WANT TO LIVE IN A RADICAL CHRISTIAN COMMUNITY?

Check out some of the things springing up around the new monasticism (<www.newmonasticism.org>) and the communities growing up around the 24-7 prayer movement (<www.boiler-rooms.com/cm/>).

WHAT CAN I DO IF I AM NOT CALLED TO LIVE IN A SLUM COMMUNITY?

You may feel you are not called and equipped to live the life of a new friar, yet something within you was awakened as you read about their lives. You can still live in solidarity with the poor, and in support of the new friars. Many of the new friar communities offer unique partnerships on their websites for those not living in their urban poor communities. Embracing their lifestyle disciplines, visiting a team for a short time to offer a specific skill, praying regularly, giving financially and adopting a simple lifestyle in deference to the poor are just some of the ways you can support this movement. Putting yourself in real proximity to people in need is not difficult. Binding the lives of the nonpoor together with the lives of the poor is more of a challenge. To start, look over these ideas on simple living that were compiled by Daphne Eck of Word Made Flesh and appeared in their excellent quarterly magazine, *The Cry*.

SUGGESTIONS FOR SIMPLE LIVING

Simplicity is voluntary, free, uncluttered, natural, creative, authentic, focused, margined, disciplined, diligent, healthful.

Simplicity is *not* easy, legalistic, proud, impoverished, ascetic, neurotic, ignorant, escapist.

RELATIONSHIP

Cultivate a closeness with God.

Practice regular hospitality.

Help each other, emphasize service.

Always speak the truth. Develop a habit of plain, honest speech. If you consent to do a task, do it. Avoid flattery and half-truths. Make honesty and integrity the distinguishing characteristics of your speech.

Don't judge.

Reject anything that breeds the oppression of others.

Consciously seek to identify with the poor and forgotten. Start by visiting hospitals, prisons and nursing homes.

Schedule "simple" dates with your spouse.

Teach your children.

ACTIVITIES

Make your commitments simple.

Don't overwork.

Fast periodically from media, food, people.

Elevate reading, go to the library.

Reject anything that is producing an addiction in you. Cut down on the use of addictive, non-nutritional food and drinks such as alcohol, coffee, tea, soda, sugar, chocolate.

Simplify Christmas and other holidays. Develop the habit of homemade celebrations.

PACE AND ATMOSPHERE
Slow down.

Do not exhaust your emotional bank account.

Lie fallow.

Say no.

Restrict/eliminate television watching. Turn off or mute advertisements.

Learn to enjoy solitude.

POSSESSIONS AND FINANCES
Cultivate contentment, desire less.

Resist covetousness and consumerism.

Buy things for their usefulness, not their status.

Learn to enjoy things without owning them. Benefit from places of "common ownership" (parks, museums, libraries, rivers, public beaches).

De-accumulate. Develop the habit of giving things away.

Offer others the use of your possessions.

Develop a network of exchange.

Avoid impulse buying.

Don't buy now, pay later.

Avoid credit cards if they are a problem.

De-emphasize respectability.

Simplify your wardrobe—give away excess.

Learn how to make do with a lower income instead of needing a higher one.

APPRECIATION
Be grateful for things large and small.

Emphasize a joyful life.

Appreciate creation.

Send cards of encouragement and appreciation when others are not expecting it.

SPIRITUAL LIFE

Make the Word central.

Meditate and memorize Scripture.

Pray.

Encourage simple worship.

Shun anything that distracts you from seeking first the Kingdom of God.

SOURCES AND SUGGESTED READING

Celebration of Discipline by Richard Foster.

Margin: Restoring Emotional, Physical, Financial and Time Reserves to Overloaded Lives by Richard A. Swenson, M.D.

APPENDIX B

FIVE RELIGIOUS MOVEMENTS THAT PAVED THE WAY

God is continually inspiring his people to Nazirite-like devotion, calling them to die to self and live for those who are marginalized. The twentieth century witnessed several religious movements that were precursors to the emerging movements of missional orders being built today. They are the twentieth-century pictures of God's impulse to call some of his people to a set-apart life.

THE PENTECOSTALS

In the first moments of the twentieth century, sometime after midnight on January 1, 1901, a young woman named Agnes Ozman began speaking a foreign language in a little upstart Bible school in Topeka, Kansas. The strange thing was that she had never spoken it before, and eyewitnesses say that for three days afterward, Agnes could neither speak nor write in English, only in Chinese characters. The event that brought about this odd phenomenon was an end-of-the-century prayer meeting on December 31, 1900, where Agnes asked the school's founder, Charles Parham, to pray that God would send the Holy Spirit upon her and give evidence of it by allowing her to speak in tongues. A few years later a similar thing happened on Azusa Street in Los Angeles under the ministry of black preacher William Seymour. Thus began the Pentecostal movement that today boasts more than 200 million souls in its ranks, mostly made up of the poor in the developing world.

A remarkably mission-focused movement, Pentecostals "identify themselves with the poor and marginalized, and those who suffer." While overall they lack the communal orientation of the historic orders, their quest for holiness, their attraction to the social margins, their elevation of women missionaries and preachers, and their ability to incarnate the gospel among the poor make me think they are of similar stock to the historic orders.

MISSIONARIES OF CHARITY

Fifty years after Agnes Ozman witnessed the birth of the Pentecostal movement, another Agnes brought to life an order that would serve as a corrective to the twentieth-century legacy of urban poverty. In 1950 Agnes Gonxha Bojaxhiu, otherwise known as Mother Teresa, was given permission to found an order devoted to serving the world's most destitute residents.

The first Missionaries of Charity facility I ever walked into was in a garbage community in Cairo, Egypt. The thing that stood out most to me was that the place was an island of order and cleanliness in a sea of chaos and rubbish. Even the flies of the garbage community seemed to respect that sacred space by staying out. The ground level housed elderly women who seemed to me very old, possibly near death. However, every time I have returned over the years the same women are there, looking just as they did on the first day I visited. Upstairs are the children under two years old who have no place else to go or who have been given to the Sisters by families who simply cannot feed another mouth.

Romany was one of those children. He had no arms and no legs, only little stumps that wiggled with delight when the Sisters were around. Though the Sisters lavished all the kids with affection, it was clear that Romany was the biggest star in the constellation of neglected babies who had been embraced by the order. How they doted on him! I have often thought about how hard life will be for healthy little limbless Romany when he grows up. But what a gift he has been given by these women who seem to love all the more those who are loved the least.

The amazing thing about the Sisters is that they have no illusions of their limitations. They can accept into their home only so many children and elderly people in order to be able to care for them with dignity; others they must entrust to the Lord. The babies are there only during infancy, when survival is most precarious, and then they must be reintegrated into their families or moved to another institution. Romany has since moved on, but I have no doubt that the Sisters etched a sense of honor and worth so deeply into Romany's soul that he will carry that mark with him the rest of his life. Some of the emerging friars have been inspired by the Sisters of Charity, holding their order up as an example of compassionate service on behalf of the destitute.

YOUTH WITH A MISSION

One recurring theme in the history of the missional movements in this book is that they were very often founded by people in their twenties. Each movement was predominantly fueled by youth with a mission.

In 1960 two young men in their early twenties were sent from the United States to Liberia to build a road through the jungle to a leper colony. They were the first missionaries from a new organization known as Youth With A Mission. By 1970 YWAMers were a collection of Jesus freaks from all over the world who would do anything to bring the reality of the kingdom of God to bear on every continent. In the squalid refugee camps of Thailand in the 1970s, Southeast Asian exiles fleeing war and persecution marveled that these mostly middle-class youth would pay their own way to come to their camp and shovel human excrement, repair sewage pipes and fix toilets. That "do anything anywhere" attitude marked this missionary youth order and gave them the distinct flavor of the mission-obsessed orders of old.

In a very short time Youth With A Mission grew to become one of the largest and most multinational, multidenominational movements in the history of the church. Today there are over 11,000 YWAMers in 140 countries. This is possible because of YWAM's extremely decentralized nature and the high value placed on local independence. Each YWAM base develops its own ministry vision, recruits its own staff and figures out how to fund its work. They are held together by a common doctrinal statement, regional and international leadership teams, and a commitment to the ministries of evangelism, service and training, with people in their teens and twenties clearly at the core of their movement.

While they do not share the vow-driven nature of an order, one of the beautiful things about YWAM is that the missionary inside the organization is as much a mission field as those they serve in the broader community. YWAM is one of the few agencies I know that will take a twenty year old straight out of a life of drugs and send them out as a broken but passionate missionary within six months—not a missionary with all the answers, but one who is willing to call others to join him or her on their journey of intimacy with Christ. The "salvation" of the missionary is part of the mission of YWAM, and it is that philosophy that puts this revolutionary youth movement squarely in the same camp as those mission orders we've been looking at. It's amazing to me how many of the new friars I meet have served with or been influenced by YWAM.

THE NEW MONASTICISM

When I read about the intense Christian communities cropping up in corners of our twenty-first-century world, something inside me cries out to be a part of them. For much of my Christian life I have sought an expression of Christian community that defies the often-hollow suburban life held up to us as the "American Dream." We're trained for an individualistic existence with self at the center, especially for those of us in white American culture who grew up in suburban, single-family dwellings, separate from our extended family, encountering neighbors only at a superficial level. The new monasticism, as it is being called, is partly a reaction to the self-absorbed life of material accumulation, career obsession and amusement fixation that is promoted in the West and that is now being exported around the world as a picture of "the good life."

The fact that Christians are gathering in such communities is not new, nor are the basic structures of these communities. The Bruderhof communi-

ties, for instance, have been around since shortly after World War I, and
Reba Place Fellowship in Chicago since the mid 1950s. But the new monasticism is a monasticlike expression coming from the current generation.
Shane Claiborne, founder of the Simple Way community in Philadelphia,
Pennsylvania, talks about the separation of orthodoxy (right theology) and
orthopraxy (right action) in many churches. He says, "I believe the power of
monasticism is the fusion of these two into a movement that is both theo-
logically grounded and offers practical alternatives to the world's pattern of
inequality." The people of the Simple Way community, along with dozens of
multigenerational, ecumenical communities around the United States, are
attempting to live lives of devotion and service in some challenging places—
"abandoned places" as Sr. Margaret McKenna of the New Jerusalem Now recovery community calls them. In the new monasticism the inner-city poor
and homeless find freedom from the pains of want, and the middle-class and
rich find freedom from the dangers of excess. These communities are like
domestic cousins to the new friars who are inhabiting slums in the developing world.

THE 24-7 PRAYER MOVEMENT

Just as the twentieth century was ushered in by a prayer-focused move of
God's Spirit via the Pentecostals, it was ushered out by yet another move of
the Spirit: the 24-7 prayer movement.

In September of 1999, unconnected groups of young men and women
on at least two continents began to pray day and night. It seems they can't
stop. In fact, this movement has spread with supernatural force. One of the
epicenters is in Chichester, England. In their amazing book *Red Moon Rising,*
Peter Greig and Dave Roberts chronicle the beginnings of a 1999 prayer
meeting that was very much inspired by the Moravians. That Chichester
prayer meeting grew and grew, and a following exploded from among skate-
boarders, goths, punks and those with safety pins stuck in various places.
Within months they had seen a 24-7 prayer wildfire leave Chichester and
sweep Europe. In short order it jumped oceans to infect other continents.

The "millennium monasteries" that have sprung from this movement (dubbed "Boiler Rooms") are praying communities that are centered on the principles of being authentic, relational and missional, and that share a commitment to care for the poor and the lost.

Nine days after the little, inconspicuous Chichester prayer meeting began, another 24-7 prayer meeting was bubbling up from Kansas City and has since seen hundreds of thousands engaged in prayer and fasting. The International House of Prayer (IHOP) has spawned citywide movements of nonstop prayer around the world. Theological education, missions and worship are part of the radioactive core of IHOP, energizing all its activities.

In 1997 a prayer burden known as Burning Bush International began among Catholics, preceding these other predominantly Protestant movements. And I believe there are many other late-twentieth-century intercessory prayer communities bearing the DNA of old orders quietly operating without fanfare and off most of our radars. Perhaps it is out of their persistent prayer that the new friars are being spawned, rising up as an answer to the cries of their hearts for God to show up on this planet with a fresh wave of his mercy.

NOTES

Chapter 1: God's Recurring Dream

page 14   This was 1979: Somehow, even in the twenty-first century, our family has managed to escape the draw of cable TV, without even taking a vow of poverty.

page 19   Missionary statesman Ralph Winter: Ralph D. Winter, "The Kingdom Strikes Back: Ten Epochs of Redemptive History," in *Perspectives on the World Christian Movement: A Reader,* ed. Ralph D. Winter and Steven C. Hawthorne (Pasadena, Calif.: William Carey Library, 1981).

page 19   "This two-thousand-year-old pattern": Actually, Winter also traces a four-hundred-year pattern of revival in the Old Testament period from 2000 B.C. to the birth of Christ.

page 20   "If your brother, for example": "The Rule of St. Augustine," accessed on December 27, 2005, at <www.geocities.com/Athens/1534/ruleaug.html>.

page 21   "If a mother loves and cherishes": "The Form of Life of St. Clare," accessed on December 27, 2005, at <www.poorclarestmd.org/formoflife.htm>.

page 21   "attentive to her sisters": "The Testament of St. Clare," accessed on December 27, 2005, at <www.poorclarestmd.org/claretestament.htm>.

page 23   "It was always the monks": Adolf von Harnack, *Monasticism: Its Ideals and History* (London: Williams & Norgate, 1901), pp. 64ff, as quoted in Charles Lindquist, "Remonking the Church: A Lutheran Appraisal of Monastic Spirituality and Structures for Mission," unpublished thesis, Fuller Theological Seminary, 1989, p. 17.

page 23   "The Protestant ethic": Viv Grigg, "Servant Movements: Protestant Missionary Orders with Vows of Non-Destitute Poverty," 2000, available at <http://urbanleaders.org/Viv_Grigg/WHY3DORD.htm>.

page 24   Missionaries with Servant Partners: "Servant Partners: Holistic Church Planting Among the World's Urban Poor: An Introduction," accessed December 30, 2005, at <http://www.servantpartners.org/about/intro/SP_An_Introduction.pdf>.

page 24   Reflecting on the historic orders: Ash Barker, *Surrender All: A Call to Sub-merge with Christ* (Springvale, Australia: UNOH Publications, 2005), p. 226.

Chapter 2: Pushed into Poverty

page 29   Damayan Lagi is a slum community: Michael Duncan, *Costly Mission: Following Christ into the Slums* (Monrovia, Calif.: MARC, 1996).

page 31   They were entrepreneurial.: And most likely they were white. Even if some movement has been made to expand education and job opportunities to nonwhite Americans, housing, loans and other systems that help build capital don't function as well for people of color.

page 32   Combined sales for the top two hundred: Sarah Anderson and John Cavanagh, "The Rise of Global Corporate Power" (Washington, D.C.: Institute for Policy Studies, 2000), accessed August 19, 2005, at <www.ips-dc.org/downloads/Top_200.pdf>.

page 32   70 percent of all bananas: Ruth Valerio, "Globalisation and Economics: A World Gone Bananas," in *One World or Many? The Impact of Globalisation on Mission,* ed. Richard Tiplady (Pasadena, Calif.: William Carey Library, 2003), p. 14.

page 33   "of the over 2.8 billion workers": International Labour Office, "Global Employment Trends: Brief, February 2005," accessed on September 20, 2005, at <http://www.ilo.org/public/english/employment/strat/download/get05en.pdf>.

page 33   All day at a sewing machine: Granted, one or two dollars a day can go a long way in a slum community. The figure is a little deceiving when understood by American cost-of-living standards. Still, by just about any standard you look at, this is not a livable wage. It does not allow for decent housing, a healthy diet, an education or any savings.

page 33   In his book: David Batstone, *Saving the Corporate Soul* (San Francisco, Calif.: Jossey-Bass, 2003).

page 33   Taking into consideration: For more information on this, see <www.sweatshop watch.org>, or see the "sweatshop" and "responsible shopper" links at <www .coopamerica.org>.

page 34   In fact, of the one hundred: Ruth Valerio, "Globalisation and Economics: A World Gone Bananas," in *One World or Many? The Impact of Globalisation on Mission,* ed. Richard Tiplady (Pasadena, Calif.: William Carey Library, 2003), p. 15.

page 34   Eighteen-year-old Mahamuda Akter: Jennifer John, "War on Sweatshops: Campaign Targets Disney, Wal-Mart Factories," *Solidarity,* November 2002, accessed on August 12, 2005, at <www.uaw.org/solidarity/02/1102/wise01.html>.

page 34   The garment industry: John Ungerleider, ed., "Challenging Child Labor: Education and Youth Action to Stop the Exploitation of Children," School for International Training, 2004, accessed on August 22, 2005, at <www.sit.edu/publications/docs/clea_challenge.pdf>.

page 35   That's part of the reason: Executive Paywatch, accessed on August 22, 2005, at <www.aflcio.org/corporateamerica/paywatch>.

page 35   The World Bank claims: Tatyana Soubbotina, *Beyond Economic Growth: An Introduction to Sustainable Development,* 2nd ed. (Washington, D.C.: The World Bank, 2004), p. 23.

page 36   Apparently, the American government: Gonzalo Fanjul and Arabella Fraser, "Dumping Without Borders: How U.S. Agricultural Policies Are Destroying the Livelihoods of Mexican Corn Farmers," Oxfam Briefing Paper, August 2003.

page 38   Haugen writes of Shama: Gary Haugen, *Good News About Injustice* (Downers Grove, Ill.: InterVarsity Press, 1999), p. 127.

page 38   That's how: "A Future Without Child Labour," Global Report Under the Follow-up to the ILO Declaration on Fundamental Principles and Rights at Work, 2002 International Labour Conference (Geneva, Switzerland: International Labour Office, 2002), report I (B), p. 16, accessed on August 22, 2005, at <www.ilo.org/dyn/

declaris/DECLARATIONWEB.DOWNLOAD_BLOB?Var_DocumentID=1566>.

page 41   tend to keep them concentrated: Edward Goetz, *Clearing the Way: Deconcentrating the Poor in Urban America* (Washington, D.C.: Urban Institute Press, 2003).

page 41   Every seven years: Actually, the law seems to imply that the debt forgiveness occurred every seventh year no matter when a loan was made, meaning that the maximum period for a loan was seven years.

page 43   "There will always be some": This is the verse that Jesus quotes when he tells the disciples, "The poor you will always have with you" in Matthew 26:11 (NIV). The gist of the verse is that the disciples would always have the honor and privilege of loaning to the poor, but that he was going to be with them physically for a very limited time.

page 43   Archaeologists have discovered: Chester Wood, "A Biblical Theology of Poverty," seminar given to the Salvation Army, Indianapolis, Indiana, August 28, 2002.

Chapter 3: Sucked into Poverty

page 45   "The set of meanings and values": Father Benigno Beltran, "Prophetic Dialogue with the Poor: Solidarity with God's People in Smokey Mountain," unpublished paper, Smokey Mountain, Tondo, Manila, p. 6.

page 45   "The people of Smokey Mountain": Ibid., p. 8.

page 46   Poverty, at least in part: Darrow Miller, *Discipling Nations: The Power of Truth to Transform Cultures* (Seattle: YWAM Publishing, 1998), p. 67.

page 46   Investment thinking and long-term planning: Rudy Carrasco, "Protest and Invest," *PRISM,* July/August 2004, pp. 18-21.

page 51   Sin is more expensive: I have slipped in the word *sin* without properly tackling a definition because I've been trying my best to avoid it. My next paragraph expands on it very, very briefly. But it's hard to address sin without writing a book. In fact, an excellent one is *The Smell of Sin* by Don Everts (Downers Grove, Ill.: InterVarsity Press, 2003).

page 51   Augustine uses three analogies: Alister McGrath, *Christian Theology: An Introduction* (Cambridge, Mass.: Blackwell Publishers, 1997), p. 429.

page 55   In Nigeria, for instance: Brian Murphy, "Help Sought to Combat Nigeria Sex Trade: Police Seek Christian Aid to Fight Voodoo Grip of Nigerian Sex Trade," ABC News International, Associated Press, Athens, Greece, May 19, 2005, accessed on September 14, 2005, at <http://abcnews.go.com/International/wireStory?id=772394>.

Chapter 4: The Voluntary Poverty of God

page 58   "A many-sided genius": *Empires Ascendant: Time Frame 40 BC—200 AD* (Richmond, Va.: Time-Life Books, 1987), p. 161.

page 61   "It's such a convenient": Heather Coaster, "Stay," *The Other Journal,* no. 3, Human Trafficking and Sexual Slavery 2004, accessed August 22, 2005, at <www.theotherjournal.com/article.php?id=30>.

page 63   uneducated working-class men: Peter and Andrew, James and John were brother pairs who fished for a living.

page 63   one activist-revolutionary: Simon the Zealot. Zealots were lawless brigands who re-
             fused to pay tribute to Rome out of their devotion to the nation-state of Israel. They
             looked for a political Messiah to overthrow the Romans.

page 63   a man who made: Matthew, or Levi, was a tax collector—a mafia-like trade where
             the Roman Empire version of the IRS came calling and extorted not only tax money
             but also cash to line the pockets of the collector.

page 64   "Remain in the same house": Again, the inference here is that payment was not to
             be with money but with food and housing. Jesus seems very intentional about mak-
             ing certain the disciples were paid in-kind and not with cash.

page 65   Giovanni Bernadone: Much of my information on Francis comes from Donald
             Spotto's very careful biography, *Reluctant Saint: The Life of Francis of Assisi* (New
             York: Penguin Compass, 2002). I am indebted to Spotto for the hard work of sep-
             arating legend from reality in the beautiful but human portrayal of the life of St.
             Francis.

page 65   "indulgently and carelessly": Quoted in ibid., p. 25.

page 70   "young in age": Thomas of Celano, *The Life of Saint Francis,* in *Francis of Assisi: Early
             Documents,* ed. Regis Armstrong, J. A. Wayne Hellmann and William Short, 2 vols.
             (New York: New City Press, 1999-2000), p. 197. *Clare* is a variation on the word
             bright in Latin.

page 71   "You, more than others": St. Clare, *The First Letter to Blessed Agnes of Prague,* in *Fran-
             cis and Clare: The Complete Works,* trans. Regis Armstrong and Ignatius Brady (New
             York: Paulist Press, 1982), pp. 190-91.

page 71   Within twenty-five years she drew: Spotto, *Reluctant Saint,* p. 128.

page 71   But some leaders: Kenneth Scott Latourette, *A History of Christianity* (New York:
             Harper Collins, 1975), p. 433.

page 71   In one letter to Pietro Staccia: Quoted in Friedrich Heer, *The Medieval World: Europe,
             1100-1350,* trans. Janet Sondheimer (New York: New American Library, 1961), p.
             226.

page 72   "And very happily we stayed": Quoted in Christopher Dawson, *Religion and the Rise
             of Western Culture: The Classic Study of Medieval Civilization* (New York: Doubleday,
             1950), p. 211.

Chapter 5: Incarnational: Pursuing Jesus' Descent into Humanity

page 74   "Before I was captured": "Truth and Reconciliation Commission Report for the Chil-
             dren of Sierra Leone: Child Friendly Version," UNICEF, 2004, p. 26.

page 74   "We do not even want to tell": Ibid, p. 27.

page 75   "They are so adorable": Faye Yu, "Day in the Life of Faye," accessed on August 22,
             2005, at <http://fayeinsierraleone.blogspot.com/>.

page 76   "It sucks": Personal correspondence with the author, used with permission.

page 77   "My life was unfulfilled": Viv Grigg, *Companion to the Poor: Christ in the Urban Slums*
             (Waynesboro, Ga.: Authentic Media, 2005), p. 2.

page 81   at least two years: People in their twenties from the West tend to view long-term
             callings in two-year increments. Many who go out under a two-year initial commit-

ment stay longer. My conviction is that many of these are essentially making lifelong commitments when devoting themselves to a two-year mission.

page 82   "I thought like Paige": Personal correspondence with the author, used with permission.

page 84   Faye says her non-Christian friends: Personal correspondence with the author, used with permission.

Chapter 6: Devotional: Pursuing Intimacy with Jesus

page 88   The sheep inherit the kingdom: Compared with those in the West today, the sick and imprisoned were a much sorrier lot when Jesus spoke these words. Without anything like insurance, health-care benefits or an elaborate prison system, those who were sick or in prison were heavily dependent on others. Food or other basic needs had to be provided by family or friends. This is true today in many parts of the world. Hospitals and prisons don't provide for their "guests" but rely on those outside to provide for them. Without visitors a person can literally rot in jail or go without enough to eat in a hospital!

page 92   "Well, I had my first major breakdown": Heidi Williams, Tracking the Trek, accessed on August 22, 2005, at <www.urbana.org/feat.trek.show.cfm ?recordid=136>.

page 95   Walter and Adriana Forcatto work: Walter Forcatto, "Service as Solidarity," The Cry 6, no. 3 (2000): 6.

page 98   the name Peter: Petra in Greek means "rock."

page 99   They apparently loved to collect: Thomas Cahill, How the Irish Saved Civilization (New York: Doubleday, 1995), p. 136.

page 99   Painted blue: It is helpful to remind myself on occasion that my wife, Janine, is descended from these people. It gives me pause before entering into conflict.

page 99   The Romans were so frightened: First-century historian Livy, as quoted in Ted Olsen's Christianity and the Celts (Downers Grove, Ill.: InterVarsity Press, 2003), p. 11.

page 101   "the first human being": Cahill, How the Irish Saved Civilization, p. 114.

page 101   "But greatest is the suffering": St. Patrick, The Works of St. Patrick, trans. and annotated by Ludwig Bieler, in Ancient Christian Writers: The Works of the Fathers in Translation, ed. Johannes Quasten and Joseph Plumpe (New York: Newman Press, 1946-present), pp. 34-35.

page 102   So before her daughter: See Aodh De Blácam, The Saints of Ireland: The Life Stories of SS. Brigid and Columcille (Milwaukee, Wis.: The Bruce Publishing Company, 1997). A druid is a pagan Celtic priest.

page 103   "If I had the power": Cahill, How the Irish Saved Civilization, p. 174.

page 103   "I should like a great lake": Ibid.

page 104   Many of these young Celtic: Olsen, Christianity and the Celts, pp. 79-102 (see endnote 8).

page 105   The philosophy of ministry: Word Made Flesh philosophy of ministry, accessed at <http://www.wordmadeflesh.com/community/philosophyofministry.html>.

page 105   One of the core values: Servant Partners core values, accessed at <http://www
.servantpartners.org/about/intro/selves.shtml>.

Chapter 7: Communal: Pursuing Relational Wealth

page 109   "I followed my host brother": <http://www.michaelkingsley.blogspot.com/>.

page 111   "Our workers commit themselves": Servants to Asia's Urban Poor Principles, accessed at <http://www.servantsasia.org/principals.asp>.

page 111   "I learned there was great value": Craig Greenfield, personal correspondence with
the author, used with permission.

page 112   "where they will be": Craig Greenfield, personal correspondence with the author,
used with permission.

page 114   "A couple days ago": <http://www.urbana.org/feat.trek.2002.cfm?recordid=323>.

page 114   Randy White, in his book: Randy White, *Encounter God in the City: Onramps to Personal and Community Transformation* (Downers Grove, Ill.: InterVarsity Press, 2006).

page 115   a network of thirty towns: The Jesuits called these towns "reductions." This name
was not conceived with the negativity that the English word denotes. They were, in
effect, mission towns, where the "wild" part of humanity and the "out-of-control"
destructive tendencies were reduced or tamed or brought under the authority of
God.

page 115   "How had those 'Thirty Towns'": Frederick J. Reiter, *They Built Utopia: The Jesuit Missions in Paraguay, 1610-1768* (Potomac, Md.: Scripta Humanistica, 1995), p. 19.

page 117   "chained and corded": Philip Caraman, *The Lost Paradise: The Jesuit Republic in South
America* (New York: The Seabury Press, 1976), p. 58.

page 117   In 1630 alone: Martin Harney, *The Jesuits in History: The Society of Jesus Through Four
Centuries* (New York: The America Press, 1941), p. 245.

page 118   New friars are attempting: John and Kelly Smith serve with Servants to Asia's Urban
Poor and moved into an Indian slum community with their young son, Tom. John
was a lawyer by training, so when the government threatened to arbitrarily relocate
the residents of their community, John intervened and was able to get land entitle-
ments for 750 families. These families now have legal titles to their land.

Chapter 8: Missional: Pursuing the Kingdom

page 125   "Few foreign Christian workers": Ash/Barker, *Surrender All: A Call to Sub-merge with
Christ* (Springvale, Australia: UNOH Publications, 2005), p. 99.

page 126   "Rather than feeling inspired": Ibid., p. 148.

page 127   "Some days it just seems": Courtney Steever, "Who Is My Neighbor?" *The Cry* 11,
no. 1 (2005): **7**.

page 129   "Jesus said as he was on his way": Lesslie Newbigin, *The Gospel in a Pluralistic Society*
(Grand Rapids: Eerdmans, 1989), p. 127.

page 129   a few distant rumors: Jonathan Spence, *The Memory Palace of Matteo Ricci* (New
York: Penguin Books, 1983), pp. 119-20.

page 129   a long-forgotten history: "Forgotten," that is, to the Western church. Of course
those in some of the Eastern Orthodox traditions knew that their bishoprics had ex-

tended at one time well into East Asia.

page 129 "helpful to all creatures": Quoted in Samuel Hugh Moffett, *A History of Christianity in Asia*, vol. 1 (New York: HarperCollins, 1992), p. 293.

page 129 They were Asia's missionary: Mar Awgin, a Nestorian monk, sent out seventy-two individuals throughout Persia to plant monasteries in the fourth century. Among them were two noble women, Mart Thelcla and Stratonice. There are some who believe Nestorians ordained women.

page 130 "The church of the East": Wilhelm Baum and Dietmar Winkler, *The Church of the East: A Concise History*, trans. Miranda Henry (Klagenfurt, Austria: Kitab-Verlag, 2000), p. 1.

page 130 "Supporting themselves": John Stewart, *Nestorian Missionary Enterprise: The Story of a Church on Fire* (Edinburgh: T & T Clark, 1928), p. 46.

page 130 Their missionary schools prepared them: Jack Voelkel, "A-lo-Pen: The Silk Road Missionary," accessed on January 6, 2006, at <http://www.urbana.org/wtoday .witnesses.cfm?article=35>.

page 131 "the divine fire was kindled": *The Monks of Kublai Khan, Emperor of China*, trans. Sir E. A. Wallis Budge (London: Religious Tract Society, 1928), accessed on May 26, 2006, at <http://www.aina.org/books/mokk/mokk.htm>.

page 132 "Ponder well who will": Ibid.

page 132 "Even the old and experienced": Ibid.

Chapter 9: Marginal: Pursuit at the Edges

page 136 Josh says of the people: Personal correspondence with the author, used with permission.

page 138 John fit the mold: Paul Johnson, *A History of the Jews* (New York: Harper and Row, 1987), p. 123.

page 141 Local observers say: Cambodian National Council for Children, "Five Year Plan Against Sexual Exploitation of Children, 2000-2004," adopted March 17, 2000, and accessed on September 17, 2005, at <http://www.ecpat-esp.org/ documentacion/planes-nacionales/Camboya.pdf>.

page 142 "Shyly, he asked whether Servants": Kristin Jack, "Our Friends Are Dying," unpublished stories about living and serving in the slum communities of Phnom Penh.

page 142 Estimates show that more than half: Cambodian National Council, "Five Year Plan." See also the section on prostitution in Scott Bessenecker, ed., *The Quest for Hope in the Slum Community* (Waynesboro, Ga.: Authentic Media, 2005).

page 143 "NGOs discontinued plans": The Episcopal Public Policy Network, "Coalition Letter to President: Sex Trafficking," letter to President Bush, May 18, 2005, accessed on September 17, 2005, at <http://www.episcopalchurch.org/ 3654_62421_ENG_HTM.htm>.

page 144 "As John watched": "What Is InnerChange?" available on the InnerCHANGE website at <http://www.innerchange.org/what.html>.

page 145 "Something happened to me": John Shorack, personal correspondence with the author, used with permission.

page 147 "As the settlers learned": Joseph Edmund Hutton, *A History of the Moravian Church*, 2nd ed. (London: Moravian Publication Office, 1909), p. 104, accessed at <www.ccel.org/ccel/hutton/moravian.ii.html>.

page 148 When someone from the community: *Glimpses*, no. 4 (2003), accessed at <http://chi.gospelcom.net/GLIMPSEF/Glimpses/glmps004.shtml>.

page 148 "In its singleness of aim": Kenneth Scott Latourette, *A History of Christianity* (New York: Harper Collins, 1975).

page 149 Since the Moravians were: Peter Vogt, "A Voice for Themselves: Women as Participants in Congregational Discourse in the Eighteenth Century Moravian Movement," in *Women Preachers and Prophets Through Two Millennia of Christianity*, ed. Beverly Mayne Kienzle and Pamela Walker (Berkeley: University of California Press, 1998), pp. 227-47.

page 149 Anna began her reign: Hutton, *A History of the Moravian Church*, pp. 118-19.

page 150 "So as not to be a burden": John Carter, "The Moravians at Shamokin," *The Northumberland County Historical Society Proceedings and Addresses*, vol. 9, May 1, 1937.

page 150 Shortly after Zinzendorf's and Anna's deaths: Beverly Prior Smaby, "Moravian Women During the 18th Century," in *A Companion Supplement to Count Zinzendorf* (Gateway Films/Vision Video, 2001), p. 19.

page 151 The great evangelical abolitionist: J. C. S. Mason, *The Moravian Church and the Missionary Awakening in England: 1760–1800* (Suffolk, U.K.: Boydell Press, 2001), p. 124.

page 151 In fact, like the Jesuits: Ibid., p. 157.

page 151 In June of 1734: For an account of the Moravian church including their mission in the West Indies, see J. Taylor Hamilton and Kenneth Hamilton's *History of the Moravian Church: The Renewed Unitas Fratrum, 1722–1957* (Bethlehem, Penn.: Interprovincial Board of Christian Education, Moravian Church in America, 1967).

page 153 "Here black and white Brethren": Jon Sensbach, *A Separate Canaan: The Making of an Afro-Moravian World in North Carolina, 1765–1840* (Chapel Hill: University of North Carolina Press, 1998), p. 121.

page 153 Naturally, plantation owners: Richard Dunn, *Moravian Missionaries at Work in a Jamaican Slave Community, 1754–1835*, The James Ford Bell Lectures, no. 32 (1994): 5.

page 153 "saw the Moravians": Ibid., p. 5.

page 153 "I do not think": Lloyd Cook, personal correspondence with the author, used with permission.

Chapter 10: Our Darkest Hour

page 155 One author suggests: Thomas Cahill, *How the Irish Saved Civilization* (New York: Doubleday, 1995).

page 155 Fifty years before: Kenneth Scott Latourette, *A History of Christianity* (New York: Harper Collins, 1975), p. 638.

page 157 "The late 20th Century": Michel Chossudovsky, "Global Poverty in the Late 20th Century," Heise Online, May 20, 1998, accessed on September 19, 2005, at <http://www.heise.de/tp/r4/artikel/6/6099/1.html>.

page 157 There are *quantitatively* more: All right, all right I hear you. The same numbers game can be played in the other direction, saying that there have never been more people on earth living in financial security. My point is that we are facing some new challenges when considering the volume of poverty on our planet. Dealing with one million poorly housed impoverished souls is quite a different ballgame than dealing with one billion or more people on the very edge of survival.

page 157   2.7 billion people: For the latest figures and debates about how poverty is measured, go to PovertyNet on the World Bank's website at <http://web.worldbank.org/WBSITE/EXTERNAL/TOPICS/EXTPOVERTY/0,menuPK:336998~pagePK:149018~piPK:149093~theSitePK:336992,00.html>.

page 157   97 percent of Uganda: Population Reference Bureau's 2005 World Population Data Sheet, accessed on September 20, 2005, at <http://www.prb.org/Template.cfm?Section=PRB&template=/Content/ContentGroups/Datasheets/2005_World_Population_Data_Sheet.htm>.

page 158   128 species: Howard Youth, *Winged Messengers: The Decline of Birds*, Worldwatch Papers, ed. Thomas Prugh, no. 165 (Washington, D.C.: Worldwatch Institute, March 2003), p. 5.

page 159   Apparently a small coastal village: Chester Wood, "A Biblical Theology of Poverty," seminar given to the Salvation Army, Indianapolis, Indiana, August 28, 2002.

page 160   "My name is Ricardo": Jenny Smith, "Ricardo: 'The only thing I hate in the world is the police,'" *New Internationalist*, no. 377, April 2005, accessed May 26, 2006, at <www.newint.org/index4.html>.

page 161   over 100 million: See "U.S. Congress Cites Growing World Problem of 'Street Children,'" by Jim Fisher-Thompson, accessed at <http://usinfo.state.gov/gi/Archive/2005/Sep/16-723661.html>.

page 161   the global population of those: See the U.S. Census Bureau's "Global Population Profile: 2002," accessed at <http://www.census.gov/ipc/www/wp02.html>. Look for "Global Population Composition," p. 7.

page 161   *Lord of the Flies*: A 1954 novel by William Golding in which a group of boys stranded on an island degenerate into a barbaric society where anarchy and brutality rule.

page 161   At the start of the twenty-first century: UNICEF, "Child Labour Today" (2005), p. 28.

page 161   "Her eyes are made up": Jocasta Shakespeare, "Saving the Child Sex Slaves," accessed on September 22, 2005, at <http://www.burmalibrary.org/reg.burma/archives/199406/msg00057>.

page 162   Today the number of children: UNICEF, "Childhood Under Threat: The State of the World's Children 2005." For more information see <http://www.unicef.org>.

page 162   During the twentieth century: Jane Peterson, "Reinventing Cities for People and the Planet," Worldwatch Paper 147, Worldwatch Institute (June 1999): 5.

page 162   But as the colonial machine wound down: This is a huge oversimplification. For a brief historical overview on the emergence of cities check out just about any decent world history book. *A History of World Societies,* 5th ed., edited by John McKay, B. D. Hill, J. Buckler and P. B. Ebrey has a great chapter on the emergence of the "Third World." I included this chapter in a reader I assembled to give students an idea of the complexity of urban transformation: *The Quest for Hope in the Slum Community* (Waynesboro, Ga.: Authentic Media, 2005).

page 165 Genocide is the systematic: Samuel Totten, William Parsons and Israel Charney, eds., *Century of Genocide: Eyewitness Accounts and Critical Views* (New York: Garland Publishing, 1997).

page 165 "The day that two army corps": Quoted in Sven Tägil, "War and Peace in the Thinking of Alfred Nobel," accessed at <http://nobelprize.org/nobel/alfred-nobel/ biographical/tagil/index.html>.

page 165 One researcher estimates: Vincent Kavaloski, "Movement Toward Peace in the Twentieth Century: Internationalists and Transnationalists," *Journal for the Study of Peace and Conflict* (1999-2000), accessed on May 15, 2006, at <http://jspc .library.wisc.edu/issues/1999-2000/contents.html>.

page 166 Morris Berman, in his book: Morris Berman, *The Twilight of American Culture* (New York: W. W. Norton, 2000).

Conclusion

page 167 his *Abba:* Jesus used the word *Abba* to refer to his father; it was the term a child might use.

page 168 Cultural anthropologist Bruce Malina: Bruce Malina and Richard Rohrbaugh, *Social Science Commentary on the Synoptic Gospels* (Minneapolis: Fortress Press, 1992), pp. 243-44.

page 170 "When Christ calls a man": Dietrich Bonhoeffer, *The Cost of Discipleship* (New York: MacMillan, 1963), p. 89.

Appendix A: How to Join the New Friars

page 178 "We will build relationships": Servants to Asia's Urban Poor strategy statement, accessed on September 16, 2005, at <www.servantsasia.org/strategies.asp>.

page 179 "We were a fledgling organization": Daphne Eck, in her Letter from the Editor, *The Cry* 10, no. 4 (Winter 2004).

page 181 Suggestions for Simple Living: Daphne Eck, *The Cry* 11, no. 3 (2005): 5.

Appendix B: Five Religious Movements That Paved the Way

page 185 "identify themselves with the poor": Harvey G. Cox Jr., "Some Personal Reflections on Pentecostalism," *Pneuma* 15, no. 1 (1993): 29-34, quoted in "Latin American Pentecostal Growth: Culture, Orality and the Power of Testimonies," presented by Marcela A. Chaván de Matviuk at the International Symposium on Non-Western Pentecostalism, May 2001, Anaheim, California.

page 187 The new monasticism: See Rob Moll, "The New Monasticism," *Christianity Today,* August 29, 2005, pp. 38-46.

page 188 "I believe the power": Shane Claiborne, "Sharing Economic Resources with Fellow Community Members and the Needy Among Us," in *School(s) for Conversion: 12 Marks of a New Monasticism,* ed. Rutba House (Eugene, Ore.: Cascade Books, 2005), p. 31.